CARIBBEAN PRIMARY MATHEMATICS

Second edition

Workbook 1

Laurie Sealy and Sandra Moore

Macmillan Education
4 Crinan Street
London N1 9XW
A division of Macmillan Education Limited
Companies and representatives throughout the world

www.macmillan-caribbean.com

ISBN: 978-0-230-40110-5

First published in 2005
This edition 2012

Designed by Oxford Designers & Illustrators and Macmillan Education
Typeset by Orchard Publishing, Cape Town, South Africa
Illustrated by Oxford Designers & Illustrators, Clive Goodyer & Tek-Art
Cover design by Oxford Designers & Illustrators

Printed and bound in Great Britain by Bell & Bain Ltd, Glasgow

2021
10

Contents

1 Length

Colour the longer one in each pair.

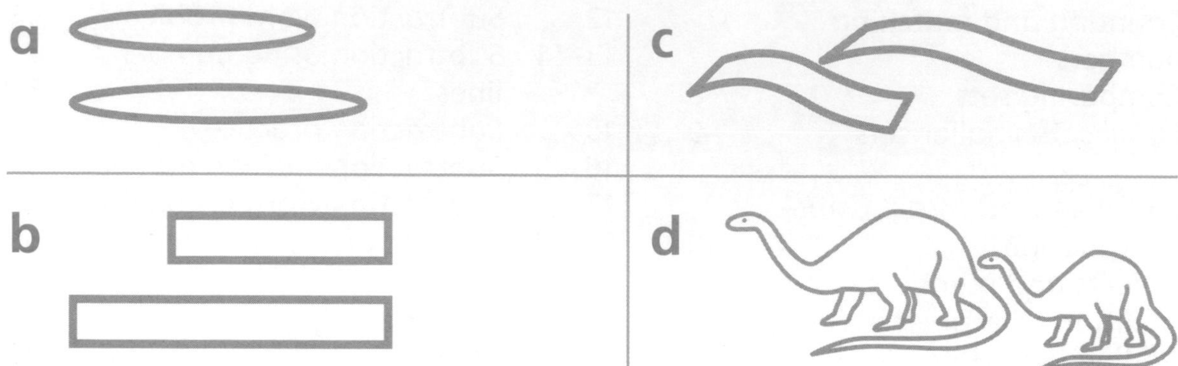

Colour the longest one.

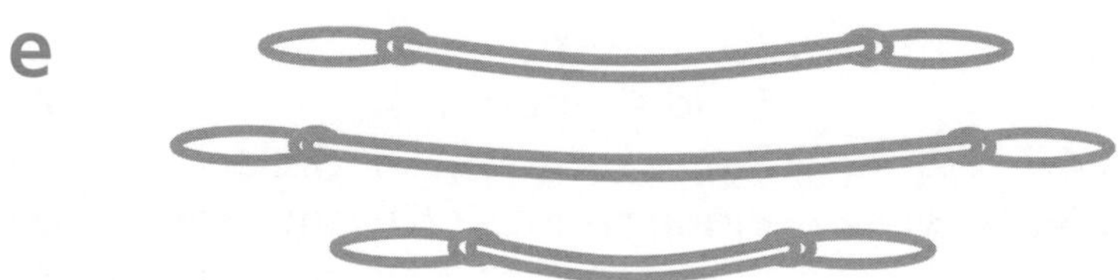

Colour the shorter one in each pair.

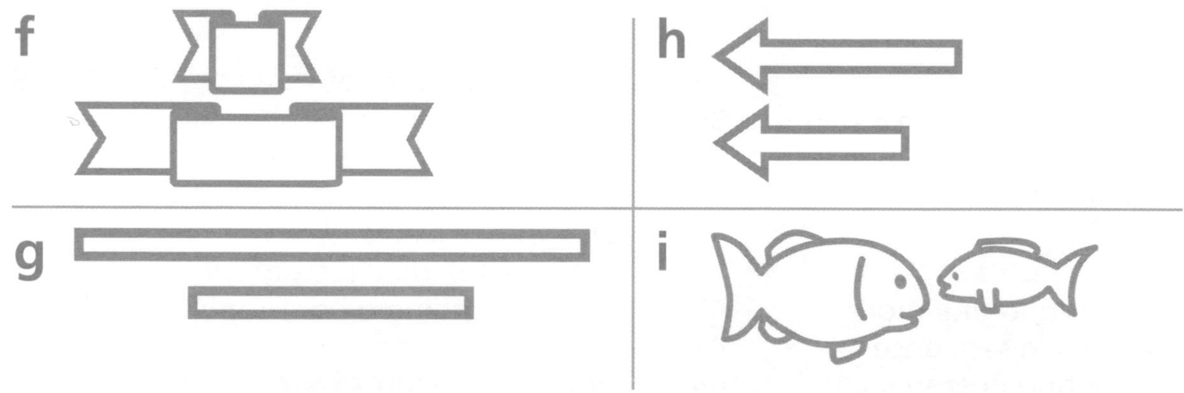

Challenge

Colour the shortest.

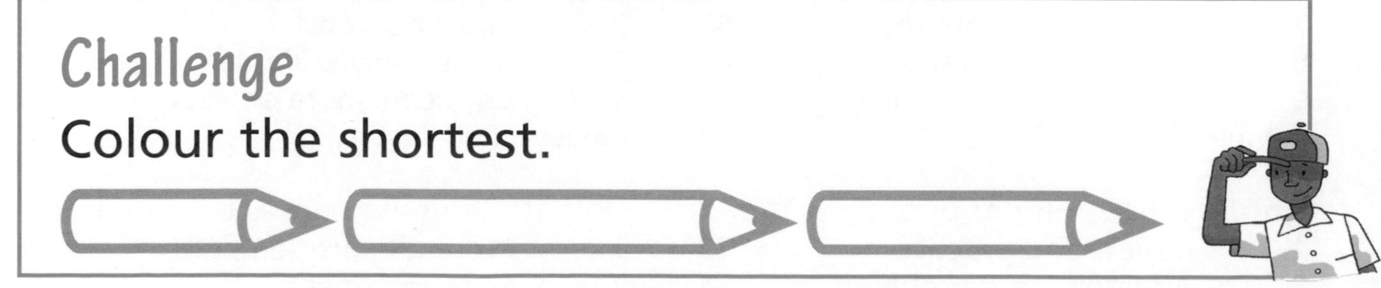

2 Height

Colour the taller one in each pair.

a

b

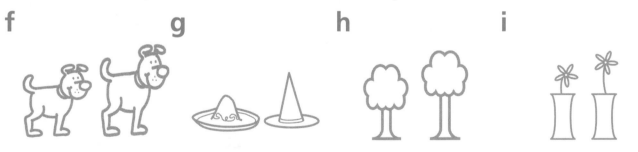

c

d

Colour the tallest one.

e

Colour the shorter one in each pair.

f

g

h

i

Colour the shortest child.

j

3 Items in a set

Colour all the stars in the set with the same colour.

a How many stars are in the set? ________

b How many stars are not in the set? ________

Draw 8 balls in the set below. Draw 3 balls out of the set.

c

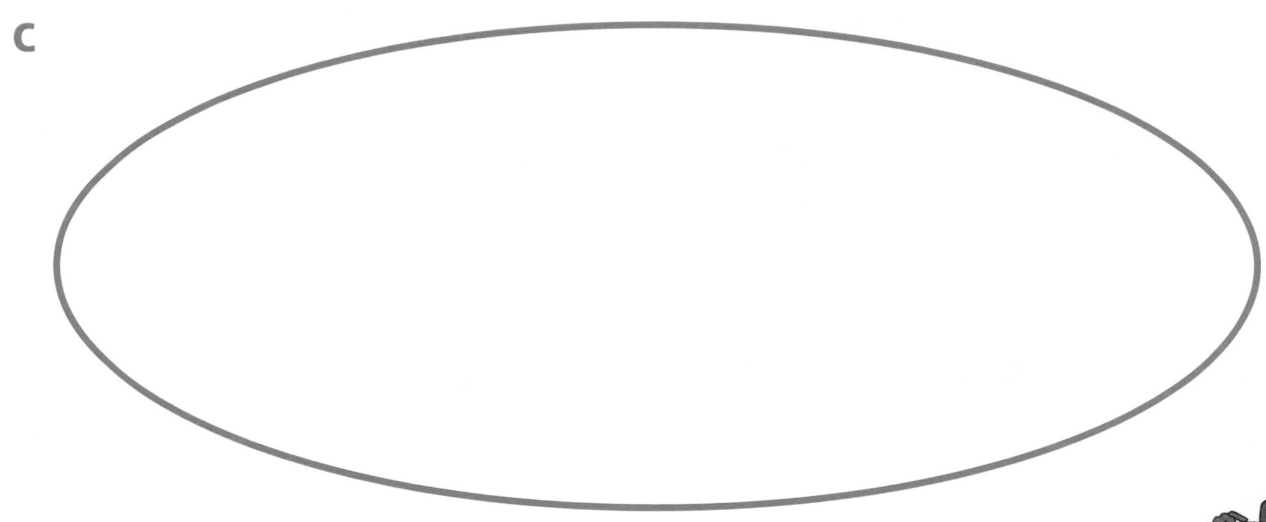

Challenge

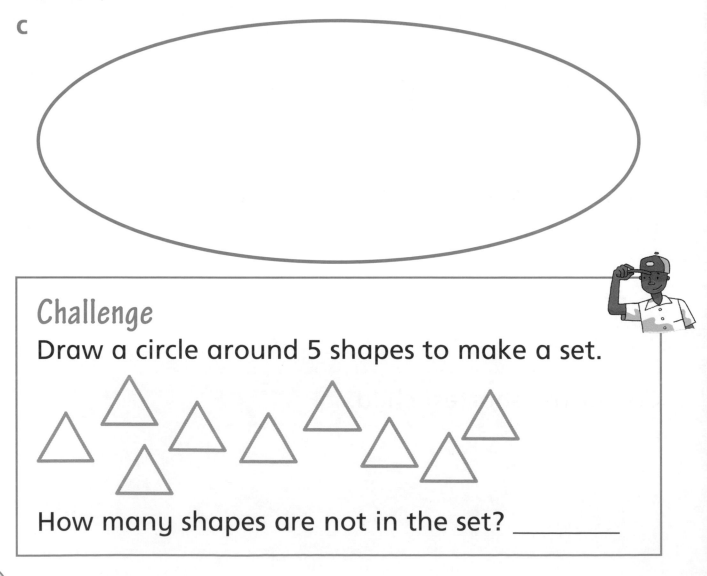

Draw a circle around 5 shapes to make a set.

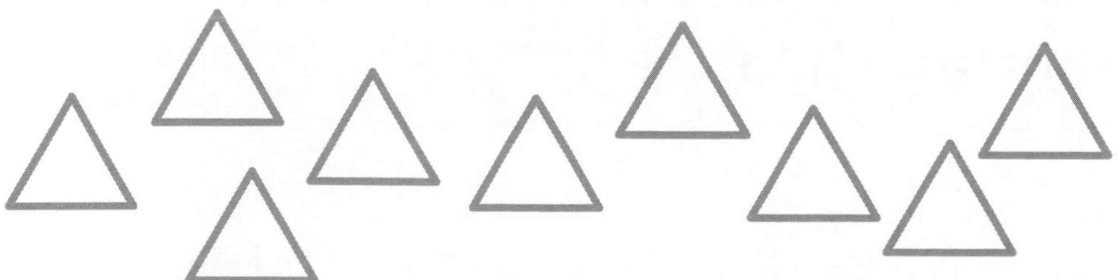

How many shapes are not in the set? ________

4 Counting and matching numbers

Draw lines to match each set with a number.

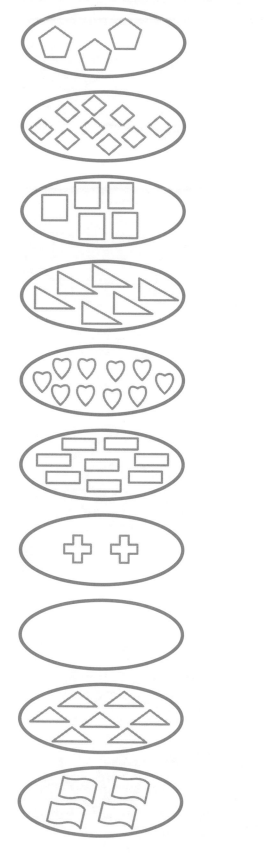

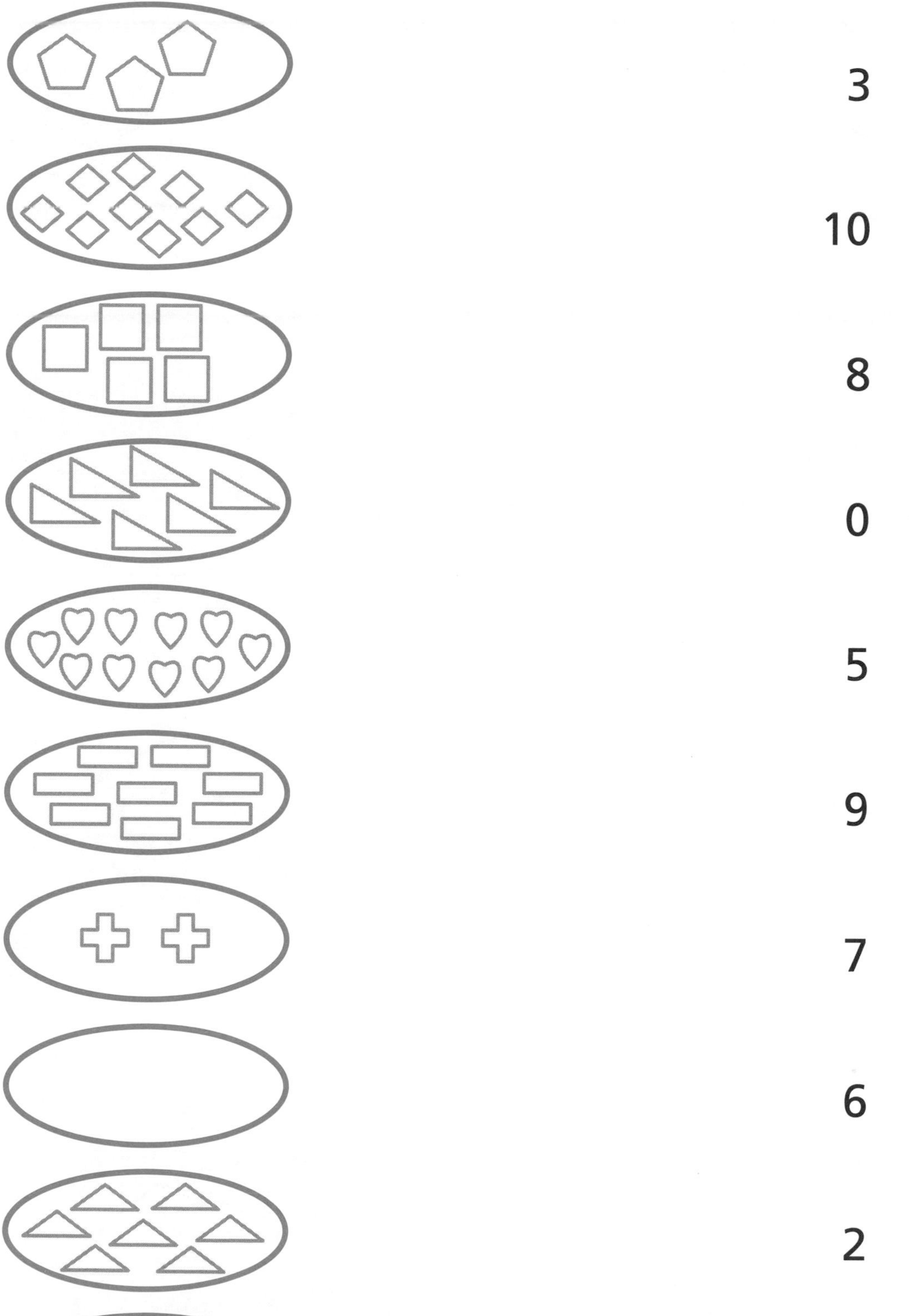

5 Comparing sets

Draw a larger set that has more objects.

a

b

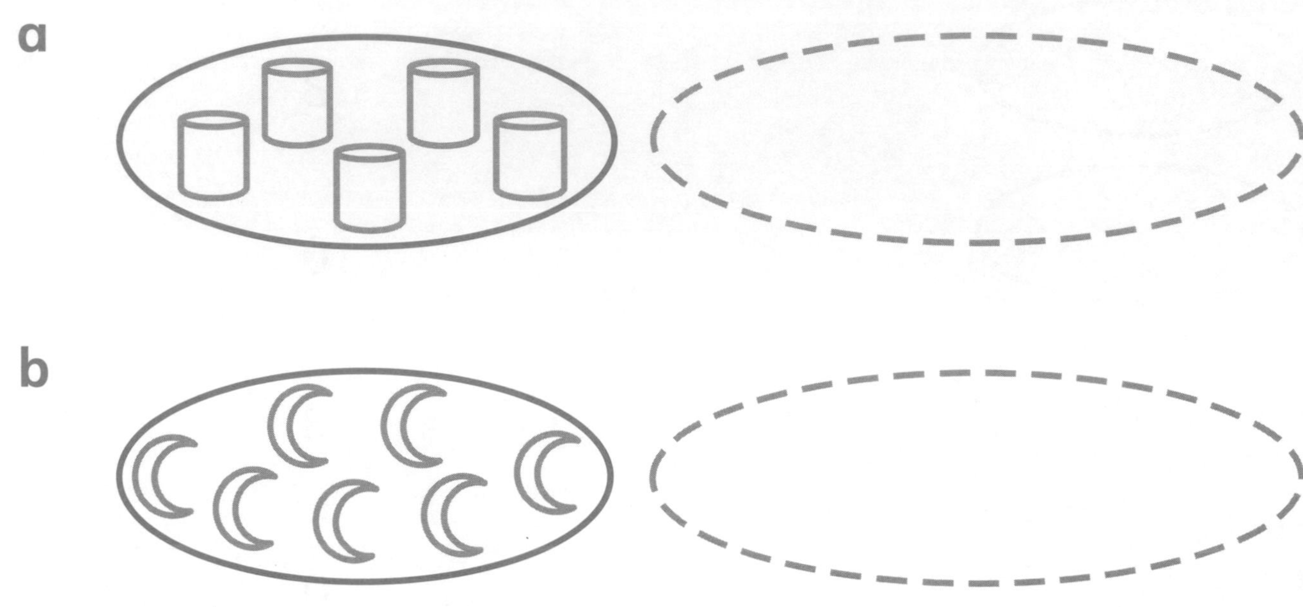

Colour the smaller set.

c

Colour the larger set.

d

6 Equal sets/smaller sets

Draw an equal set with the same number of objects.

a

b

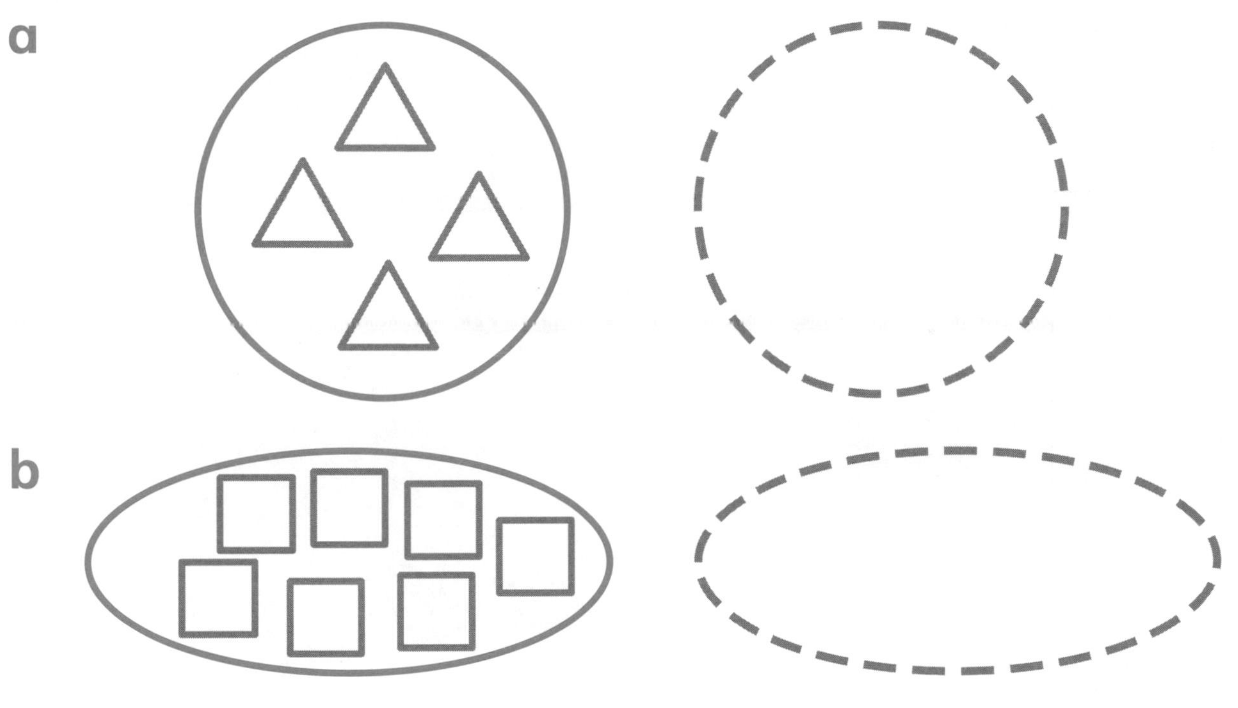

Draw a smaller set that has fewer objects.

c

d

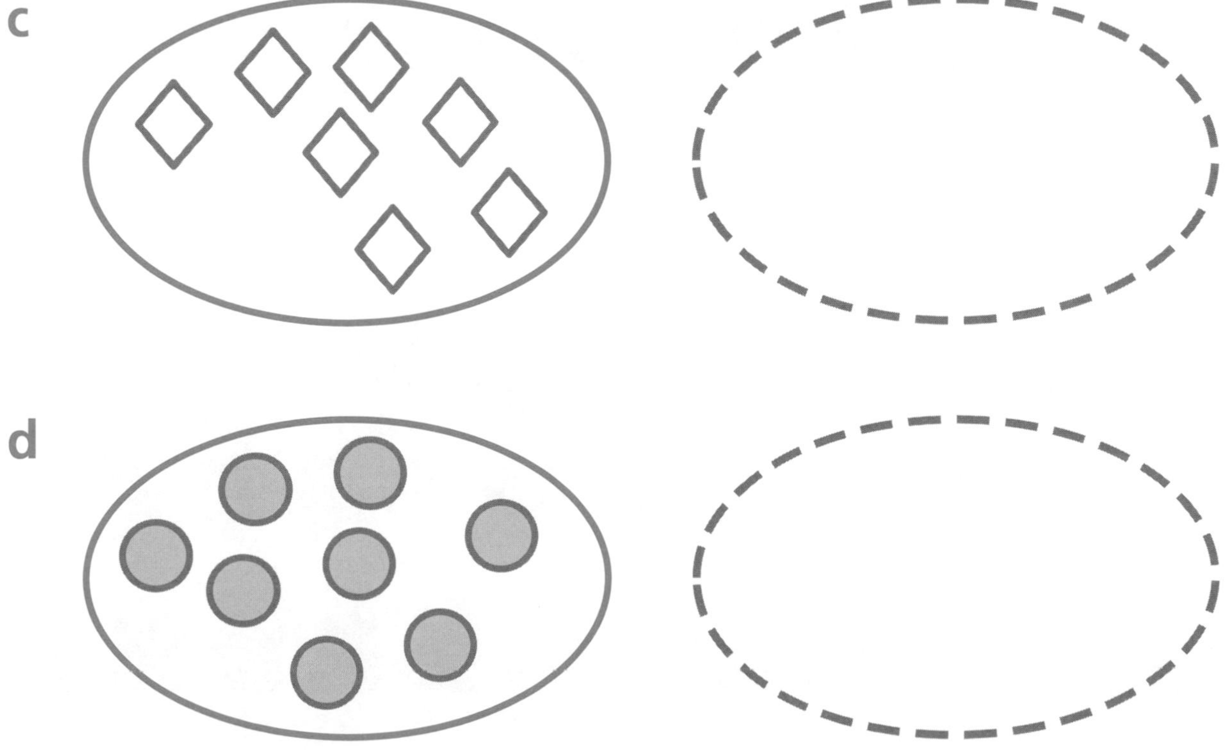

1 How many?

Write the number.

0 [0]

4 [4]

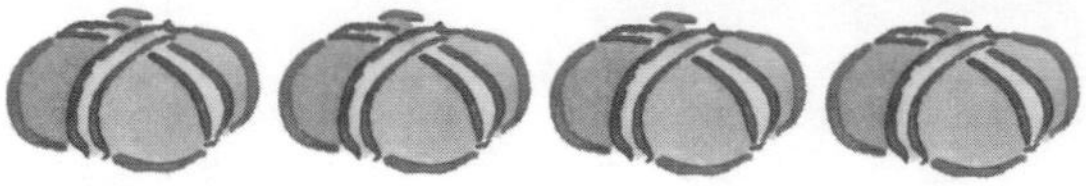

2 [ ]

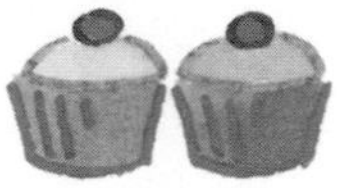

5 [ ]

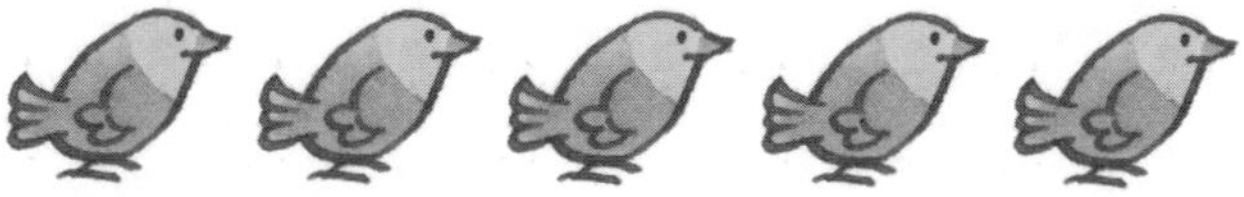

1 [ ]

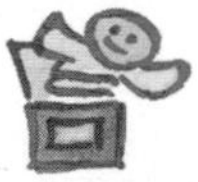

6 [ ]

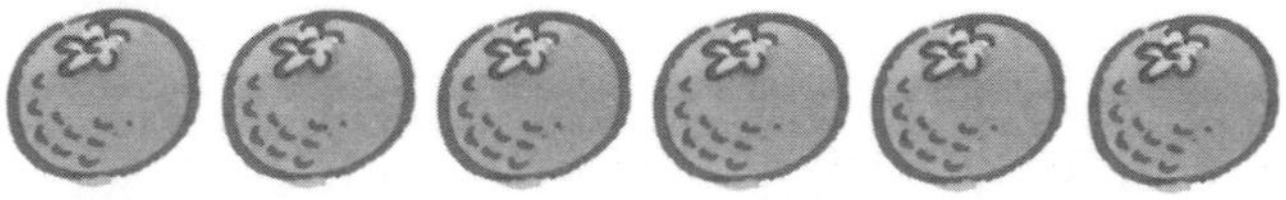

8 [ ]

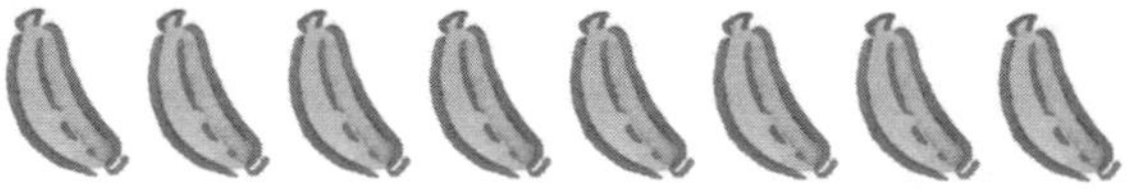

7 [ ]

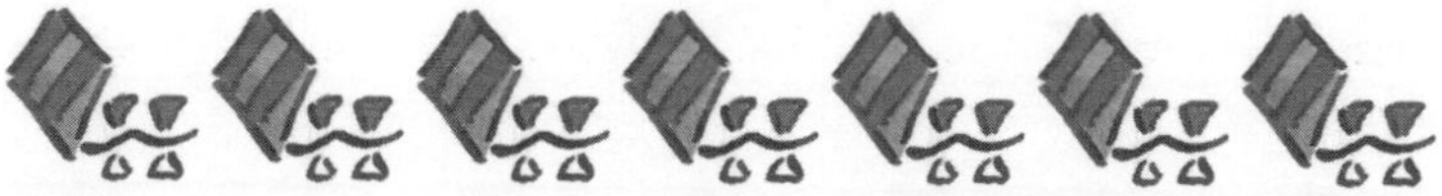

9 [ ]

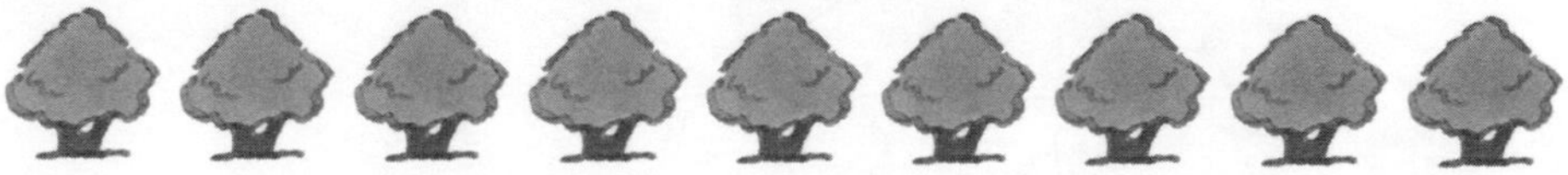

10 [ ]

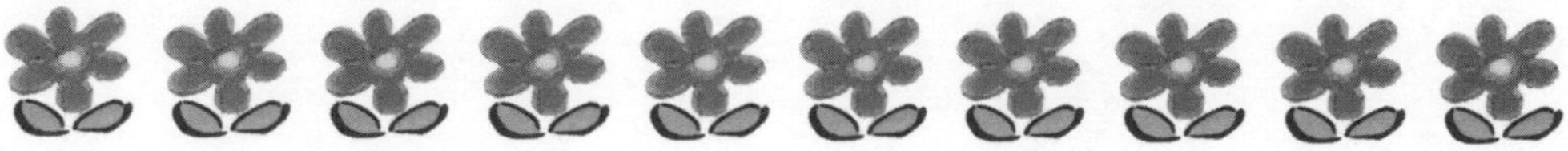

2 Objects and numbers

Draw a set of objects to match each number.

0

1

2

3

4 

5

6

7

8

9

10

3 Addition with objects

Add to find the total.

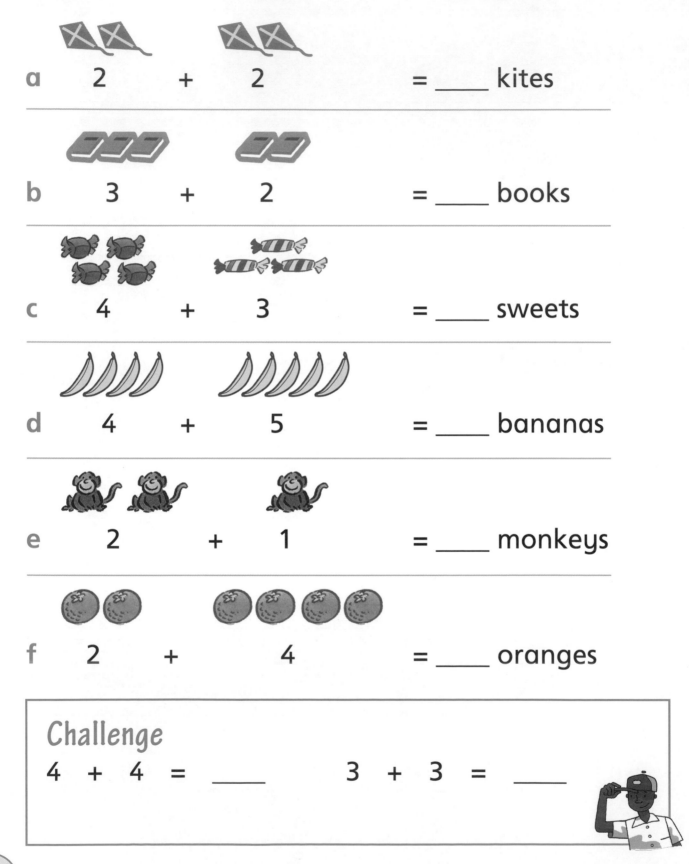

a 2 + 2 = ____ kites

b 3 + 2 = ____ books

c 4 + 3 = ____ sweets

d 4 + 5 = ____ bananas

e 2 + 1 = ____ monkeys

f 2 + 4 = ____ oranges

Challenge

4 + 4 = ____ 3 + 3 = ____

4 Adding with dots

Draw dots for each number. Add to find the total.

 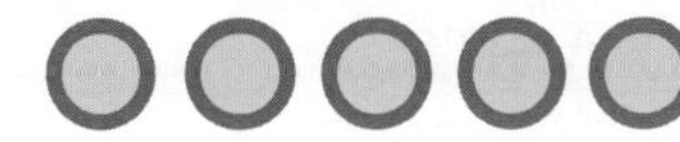

a 5 + 5 = ____

b 3 + 6 = ____

c 2 + 7 = ____

d 3 + 5 = ____

e 6 + 4 = ____

f 5 + 2 = ____

g 1 + 8 = ____

h 6 + 2 = ____

Challenge

5 + 6 = ____ 9 + 2 = ____

5 Number sentences

Add to find the total. Write the number sentence.

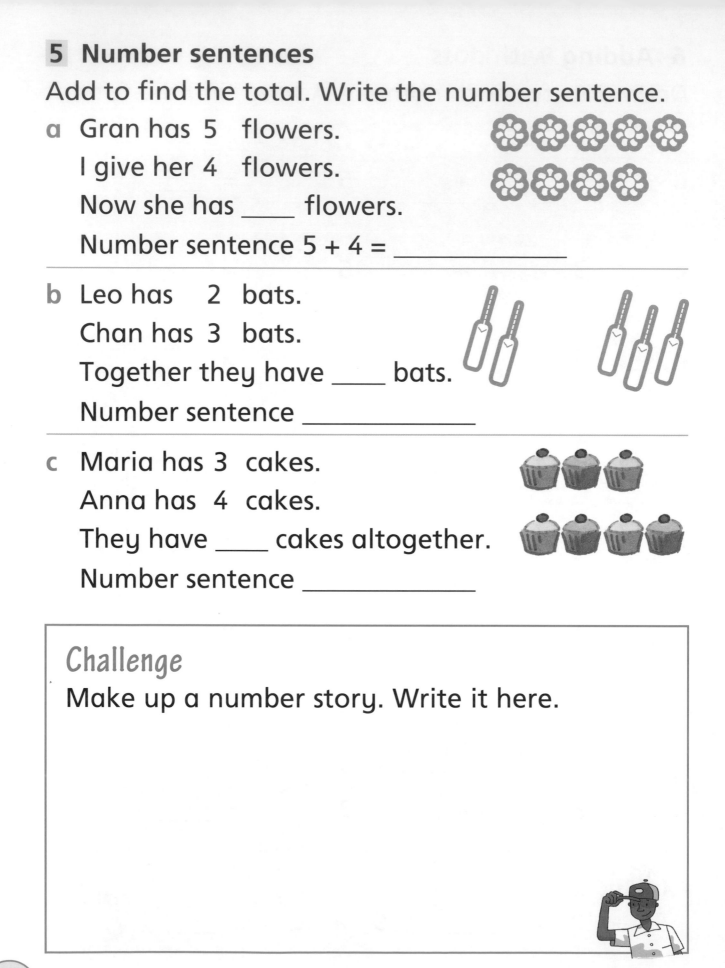

a Gran has 5 flowers.

I give her 4 flowers.

Now she has ____ flowers.

Number sentence 5 + 4 = ______________

b Leo has 2 bats.

Chan has 3 bats.

Together they have ____ bats.

Number sentence ______________

c Maria has 3 cakes.

Anna has 4 cakes.

They have ____ cakes altogether.

Number sentence ______________

Challenge

Make up a number story. Write it here.

6 Adding 0 or 1

Add.

a $5 + 0 =$ ____	k $1 + 1 =$ ____
b $6 + 0 =$ ____	l $3 + 1 =$ ____
c $1 + 0 =$ ____	m $5 + 1 =$ ____
d $8 + 0 =$ ____	n $2 + 1 =$ ____
e $3 + 0 =$ ____	o $4 + 1 =$ ____
f $4 + 0 =$ ____	p $6 + 1 =$ ____
g $2 + 0 =$ ____	q $8 + 1 =$ ____
h $7 + 0 =$ ____	r $9 + 1 =$ ____
i $9 + 0 =$ ____	s $7 + 1 =$ ____
j $10 + 0 =$ ____	t $0 + 1 =$ ____

7 Adding 2 or 3

Add to find the total.

a 1 + 2 = ____	k 2 + 3 = ____
b 5 + 2 = ____	l 0 + 3 = ____
c 6 + 2 = ____	m 4 + 3 = ____
d 2 + 2 = ____	n 8 + 3 = ____
e 4 + 2 = ____	o 1 + 3 = ____
f 7 + 2 = ____	p 5 + 3 = ____
g 3 + 2 = ____	q 3 + 3 = ____
h 0 + 2 = ____	r 6 + 3 = ____
i 8 + 2 = ____	s 9 + 3 = ____
j 9 + 2 = ____	t 7 + 3 = ____

8 Adding 2 or 3

Circle the correct answer.

a $5 + 0 =$ (5 10 0)

b $6 + 1 =$ (16 7 6)

c $7 + 2 =$ (9 5 11)

d $0 + 3 =$ (3 30 0)

e $8 + 3 =$ (10 5 11)

Add.

f $4 + 2 =$ ____

g $3 + 1 =$ ____

h $7 + 3 =$ ____

i $7 + 2 =$ ____

j $5 + 3 =$ ____

k $0 + 2 =$ ____

Challenge

Draw dots and add.

$3 + 12 =$ ____

$11 + 3 =$ ____

9 Adding 4 and 5

Add to find the total.

a 0 + 4 = ____	k 1 + 5 = ____
b 3 + 4 = ____	l 6 + 5 = ____
c 1 + 4 = ____	m 3 + 5 = ____
d 4 + 4 = ____	n 5 + 5 = ____
e 2 + 4 = ____	o 4 + 5 = ____
f 8 + 4 = ____	p 2 + 5 = ____
g 5 + 4 = ____	q 8 + 5 = ____
h 7 + 4 = ____	r 0 + 5 = ____
i 9 + 4 = ____	s 9 + 5 = ____
j 6 + 4 = ____	t 7 + 5 = ____

10 Missing addends

Draw more to make each set match the number.

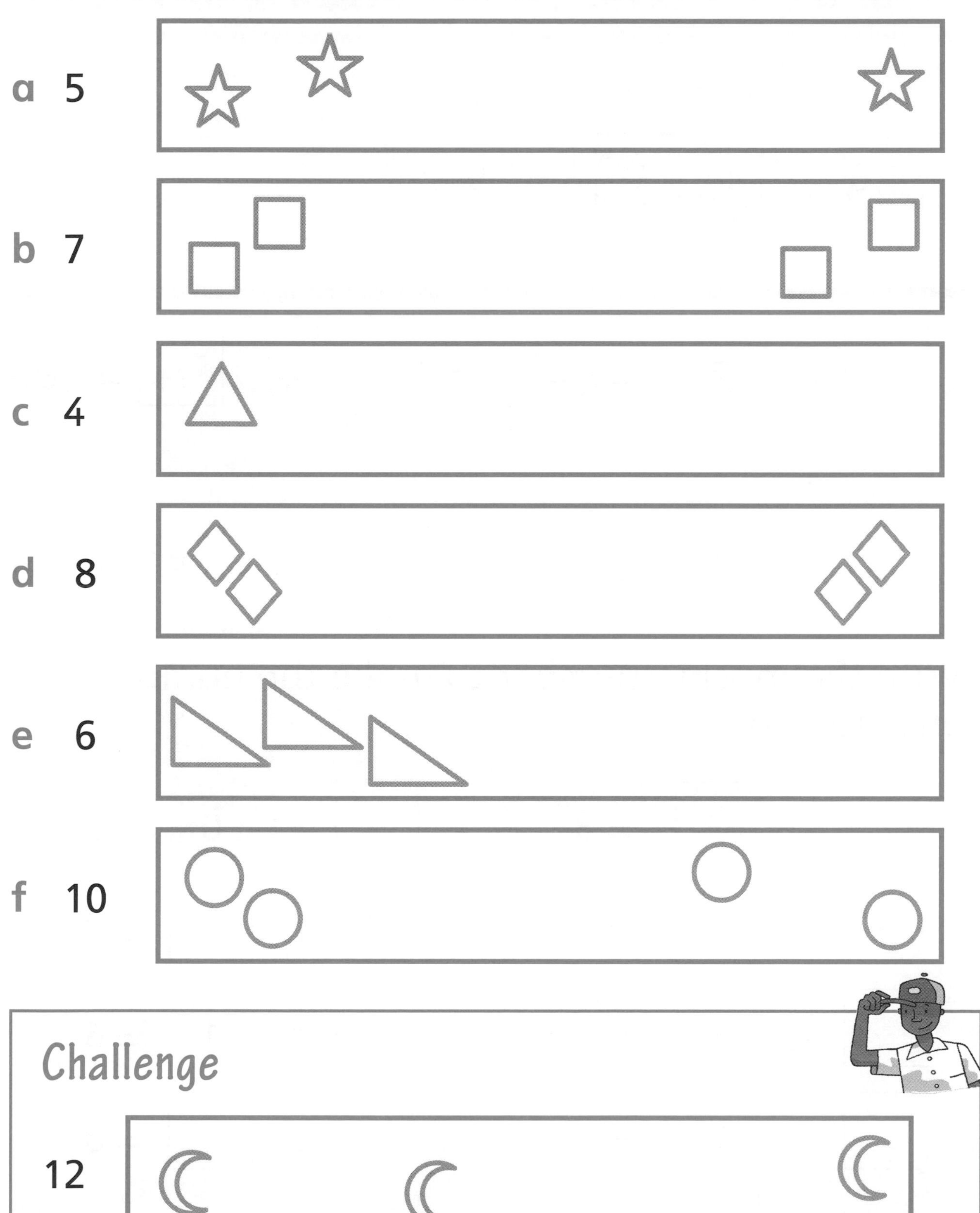

11 Missing addends

Draw dots to help you find the missing number.

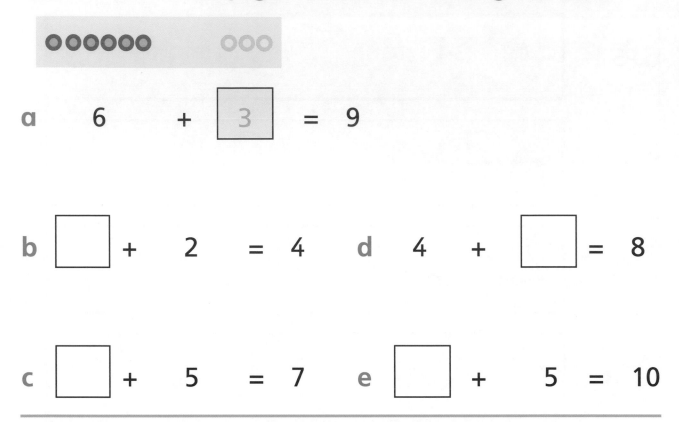

a 6 + [3] = 9

b [ ] + 2 = 4

c [ ] + 5 = 7

d 4 + [ ] = 8

e [ ] + 5 = 10

Write the missing number to make the number sentence true.

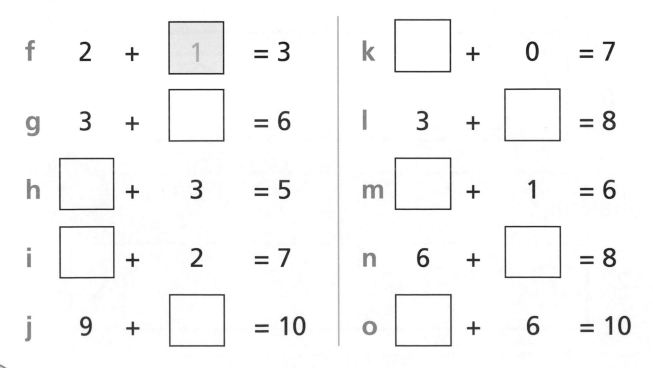

f 2 + [1] = 3

g 3 + [ ] = 6

h [ ] + 3 = 5

i [ ] + 2 = 7

j 9 + [ ] = 10

k [ ] + 0 = 7

l 3 + [ ] = 8

m [ ] + 1 = 6

n 6 + [ ] = 8

o [ ] + 6 = 10

12 Number words

Look at the box below.

0	zero	4	four	8	eight
1	one	5	five	9	nine
2	two	6	six	10	ten
3	three	7	seven		

Now write the number by its number word.

a six ________

b five ________

c four ________

d two ________

e ten ________

f one ________

g three ________

h zero ________

i eight ________

j nine ________

Challenge

What number word comes before nine?

____

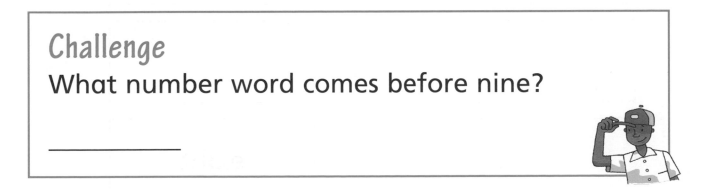

13 Number words

Write the number word that comes **before**.

0	zero	4	four	8	eight
1	one	5	five	9	nine
2	two	6	six	10	ten
3	three	7	seven		

a		three
b		five
c		one
d		two
e		nine
f		eight

14 Number words

0	zero	4	four	8	eight
1	one	5	five	9	nine
2	two	6	six	10	ten
3	three	7	seven		

Write the number word that comes **after**.

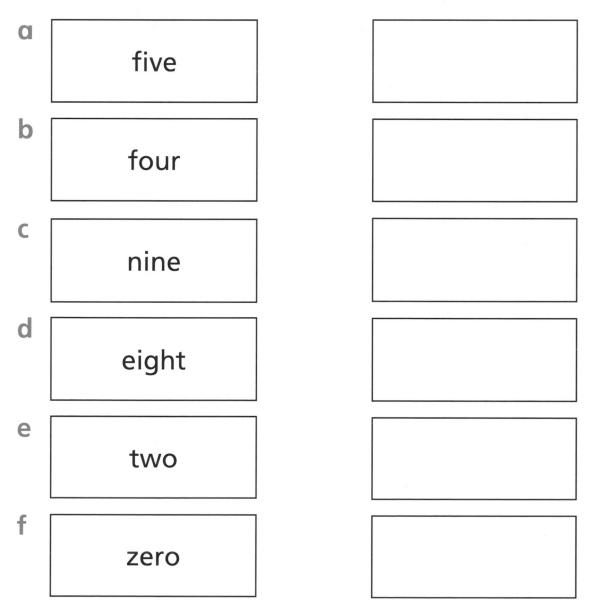

a	five	
b	four	
c	nine	
d	eight	
e	two	
f	zero	

15 Matching

Draw lines to match the number words to the numbers.

a zero	2
b one	3
c two	1
d three	0
e four	6
f five	4
g six	5
h seven	7
i eight	10
j nine	8
k ten	9

16 Adding three numbers

Count and add to find the total.

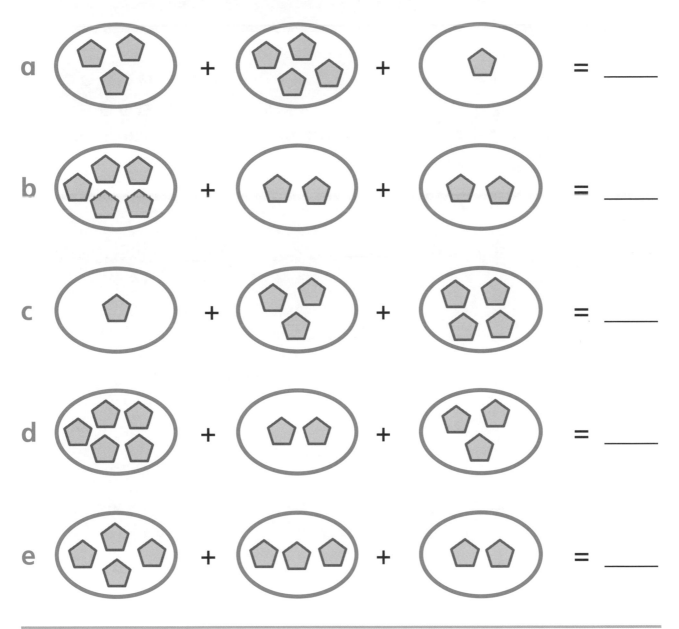

a + + = ____

b + + = ____

c + + = ____

d + + = ____

e + + = ____

Add the numbers.

f 2 + 1 + 3 = ____

g 4 + 1 + 3 = ____

h 3 + 5 + 1 = ____

i 5 + 1 + 4 = ____

17 Adding two ways

Show two ways to add.

○○○○○ ○○○

a 5 + 3 = ____

$$\begin{array}{r} 5 \\ +\ 3 \\ \hline \underline{\quad} \end{array}$$

○○○○○
○○○

b 7 + 2 = ____

$$\begin{array}{r} 7 \\ +\ 2 \\ \hline \underline{\quad} \end{array}$$

c 6 + 2 = ____

$$\begin{array}{r} 6 \\ +\ 2 \\ \hline \underline{\quad} \end{array}$$

d 4 + 4 = ____

$$\begin{array}{r} 4 \\ +\ 4 \\ \hline \underline{\quad} \end{array}$$

e 3 + 6 = ____

$$\begin{array}{r} 3 \\ +\ 6 \\ \hline \underline{\quad} \end{array}$$

f 5 + 4 = ____

$$\begin{array}{r} 5 \\ +\ 4 \\ \hline \underline{\quad} \end{array}$$

18 Forming 10s

How many more make 10?

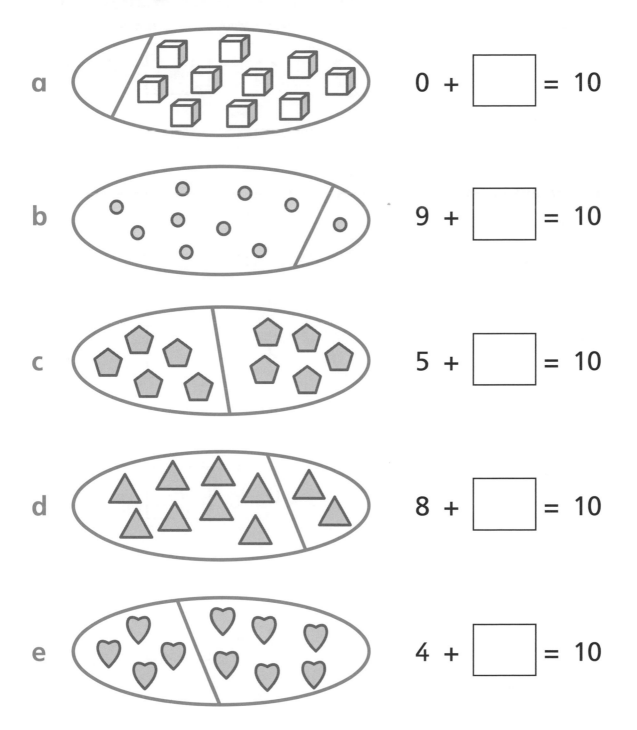

a 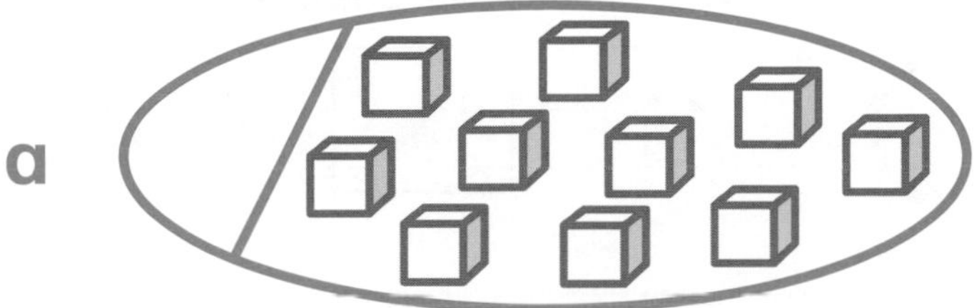 0 + ☐ = 10

b 9 + ☐ = 10

c 5 + ☐ = 10

d 8 + ☐ = 10

e 4 + ☐ = 10

19 Forming 10s

Draw more to make 10. Write the missing number.

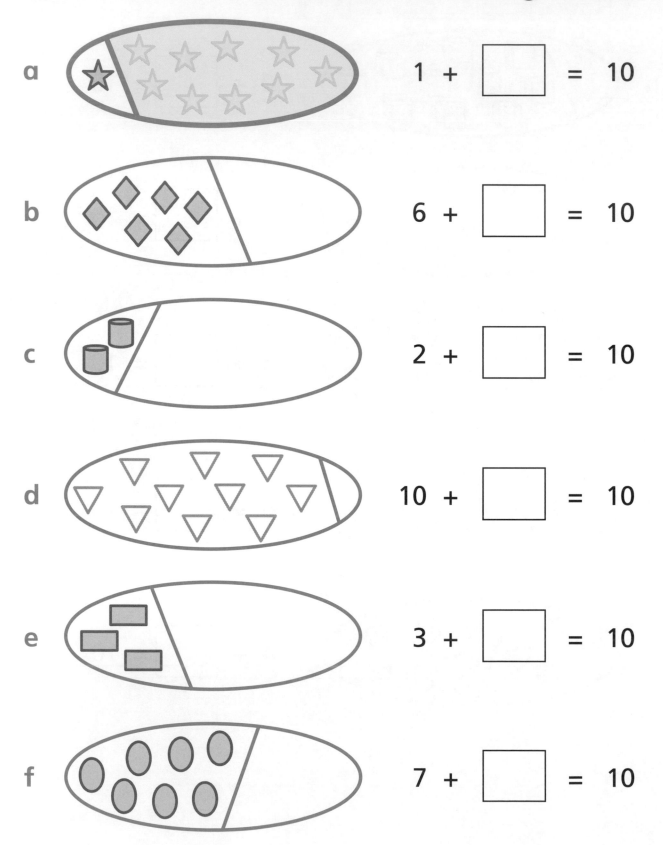

a  $1 + \square = 10$

b 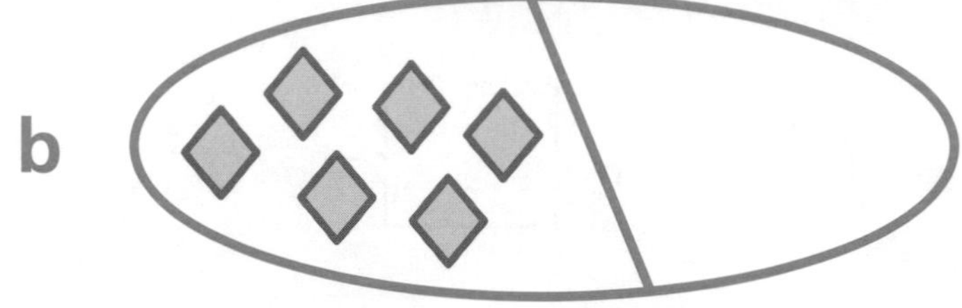 $6 + \square = 10$

c 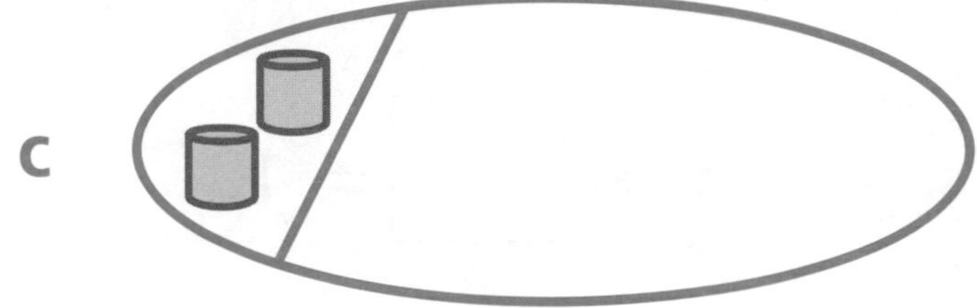 $2 + \square = 10$

d $10 + \square = 10$

e 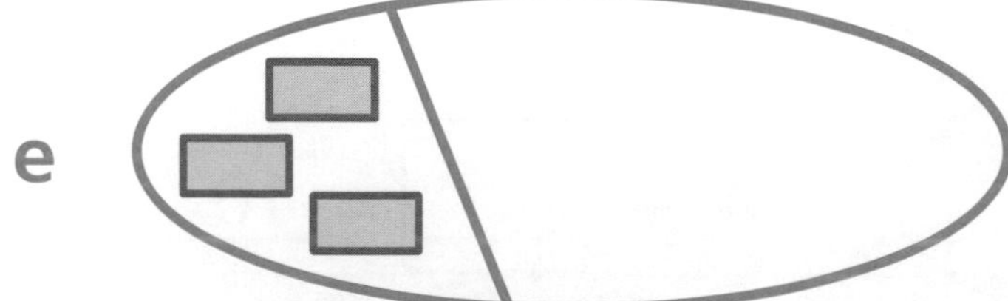 $3 + \square = 10$

f $7 + \square = 10$

Review: Self-Test 1

1 How many? ____

2 What is 1 more than 5? ____

3 Draw more to make 10. Write the number.

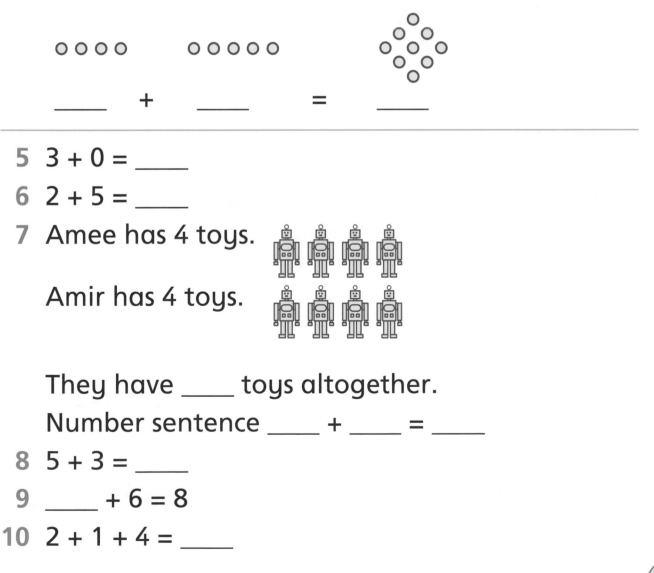

6 + ____ = 10

---

4 Write the number sentence to match the dots.

____ + ____ = ____

---

5 3 + 0 = ____

6 2 + 5 = ____

7 Amee has 4 toys.

Amir has 4 toys.

They have ____ toys altogether.

Number sentence ____ + ____ = ____

8 5 + 3 = ____

9 ____ + 6 = 8

10 2 + 1 + 4 = ____

20 Counting more than 10

Count.

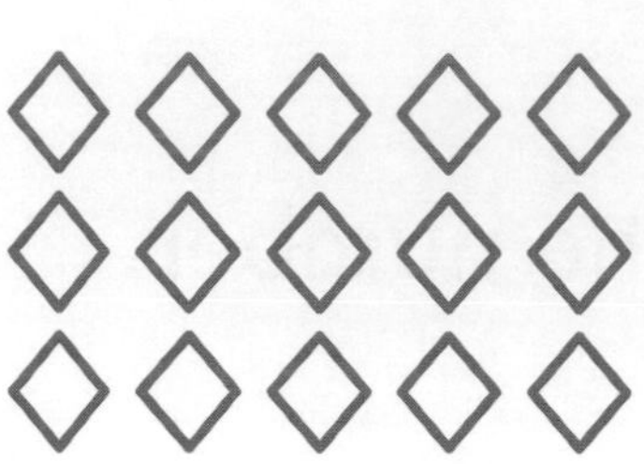

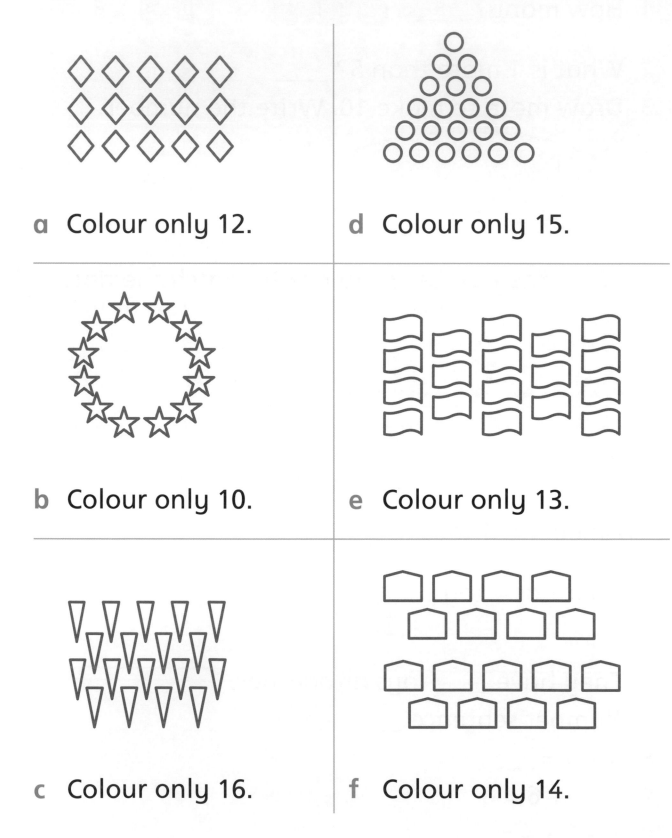

a Colour only 12.

b Colour only 10.

c Colour only 16.

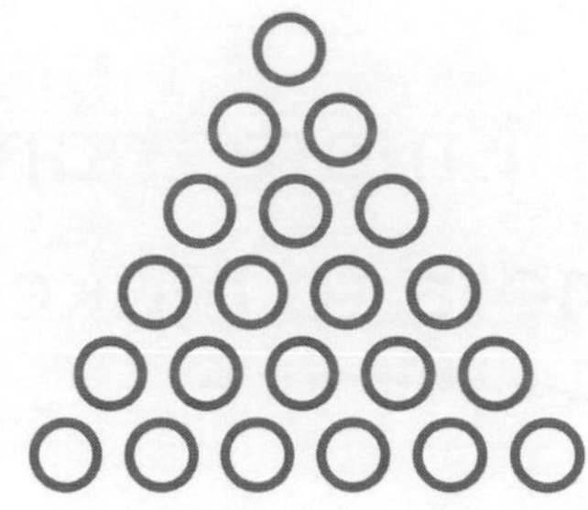

d Colour only 15.

e Colour only 13.

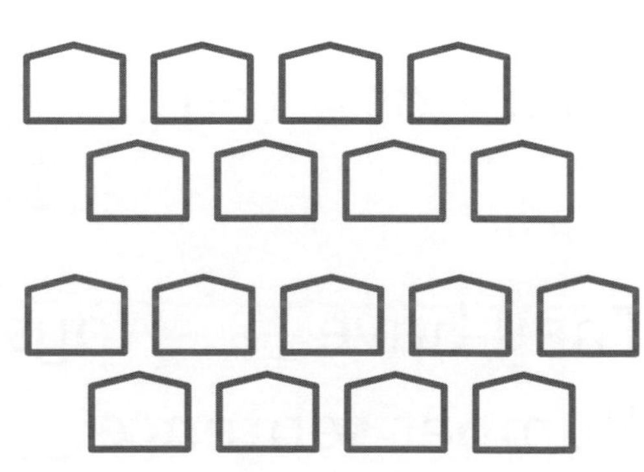

f Colour only 14.

21 Counting more than 10

Count.

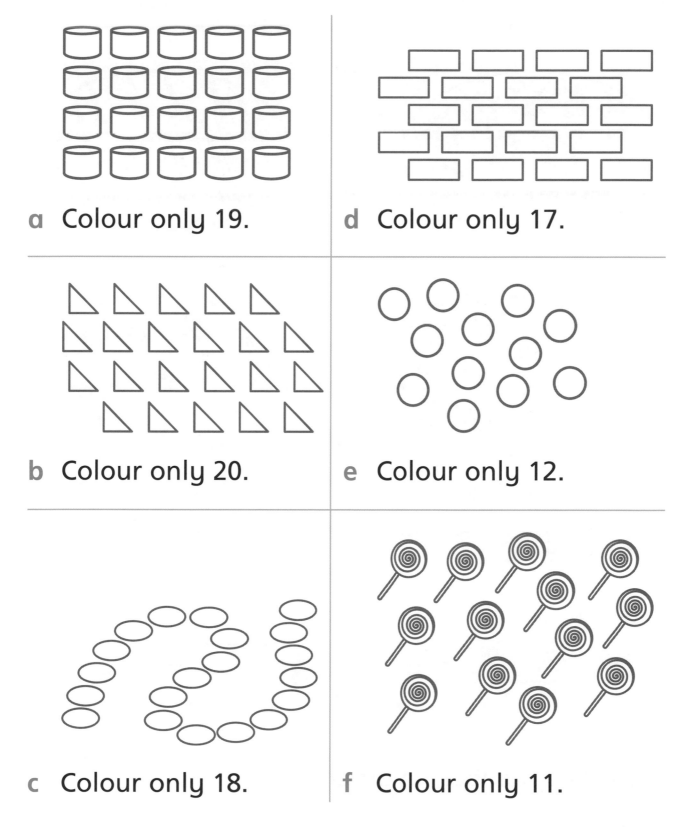

a Colour only 19.

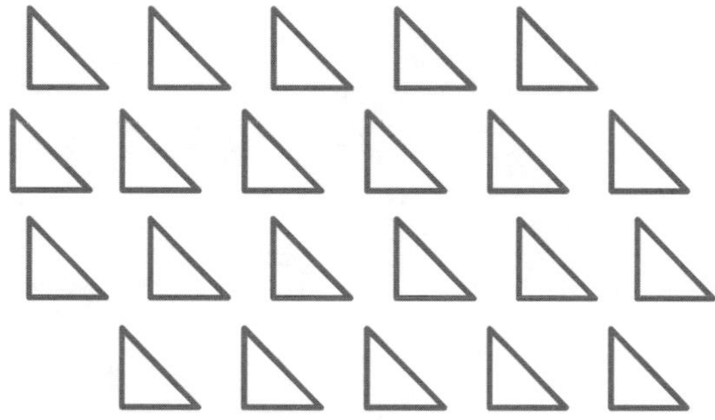

b Colour only 20.

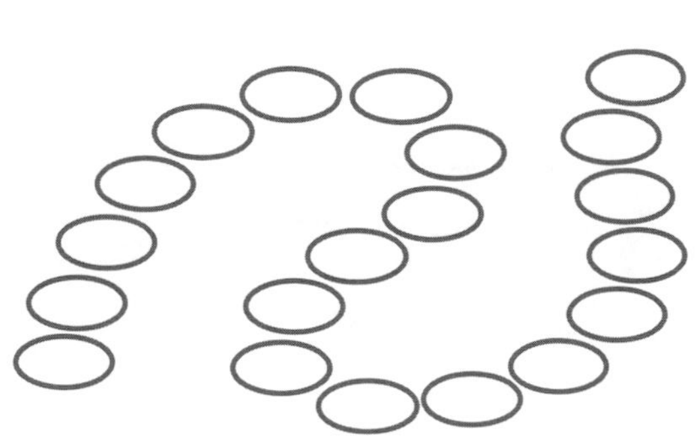

c Colour only 18.

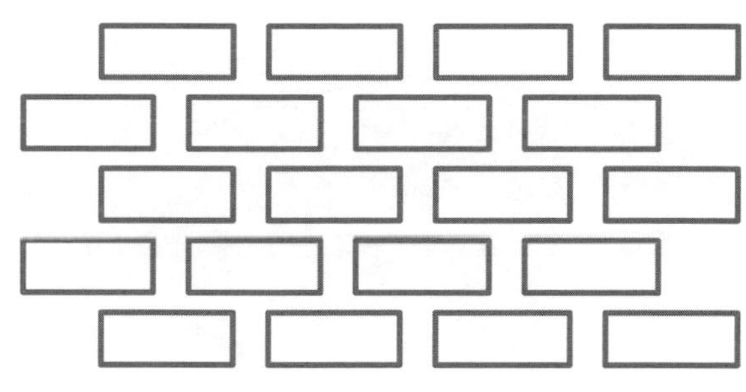

d Colour only 17.

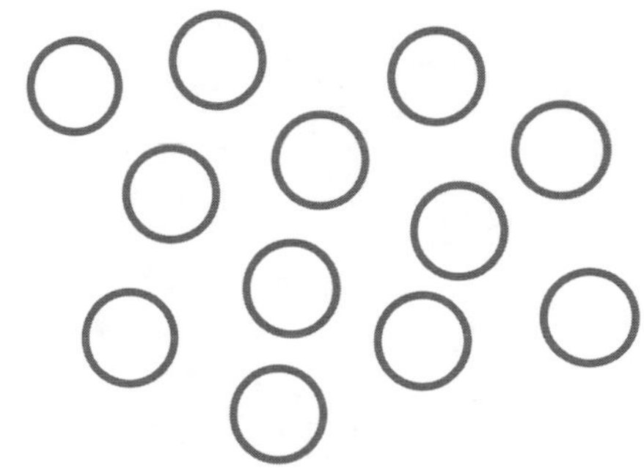

e Colour only 12.

f Colour only 11.

22 Matching 10–20

Match the number to the set.

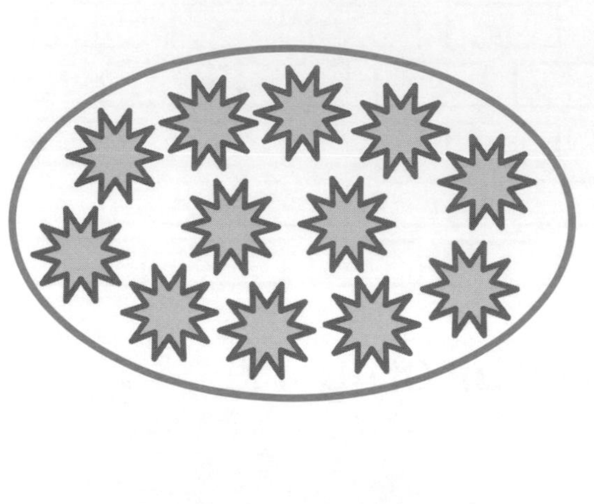

10

14

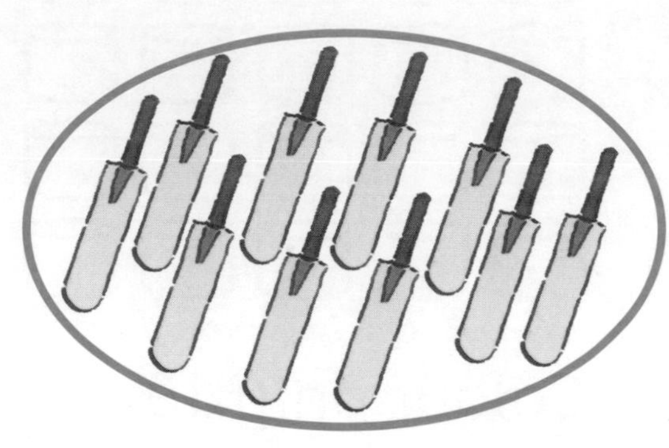

12

11

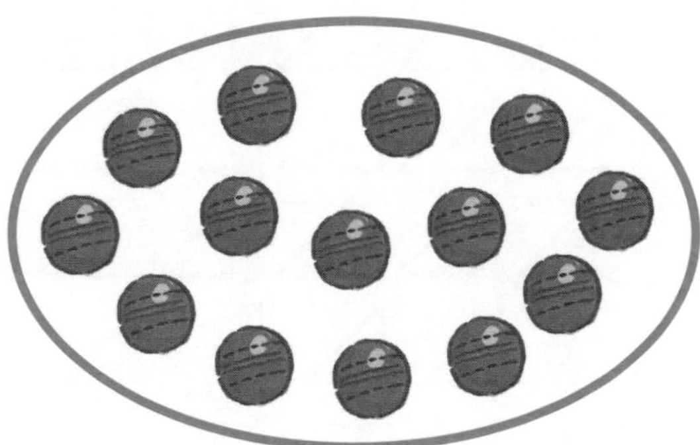

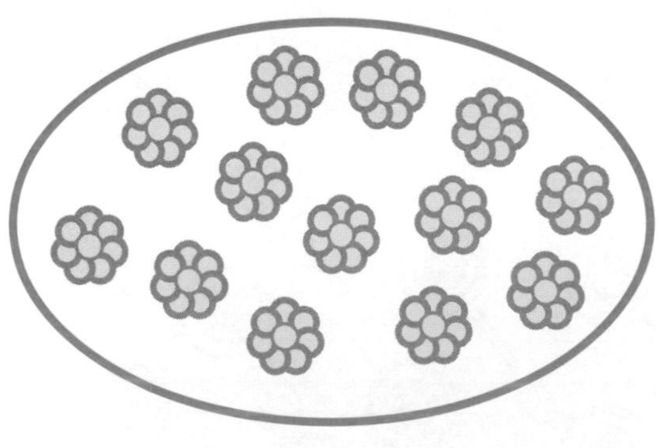

15

13

Write the numbers in order.

10 ______ ______ ______ ______ ______

23 Matching 10–20

Match the number to the set.

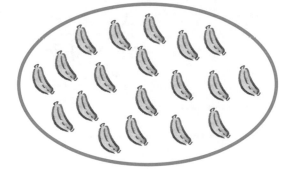

17

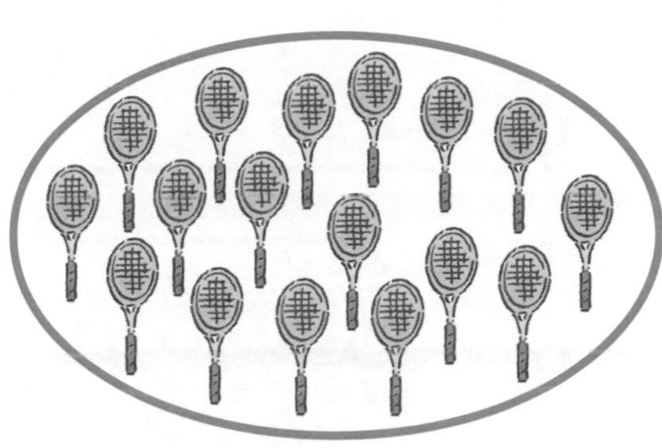

20

16

19

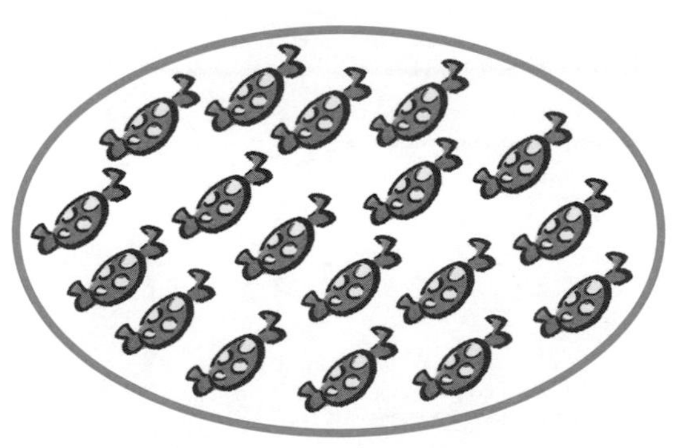

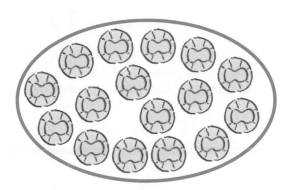

18

Write the numbers in order.

16 ________ ________ ________ ________

24 Forming 10–20

Draw more to make the set match the number.

a  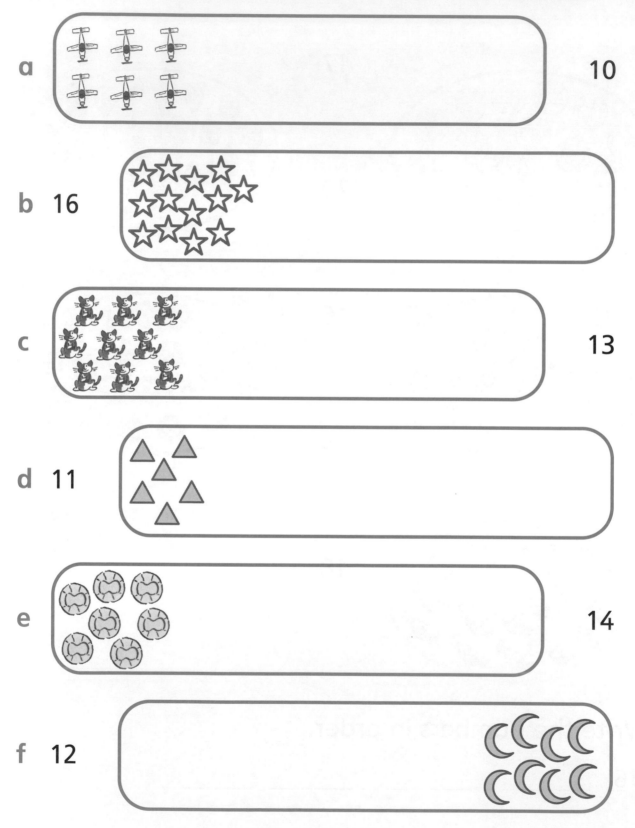 10

b 16

c 13

d 11

e 14

f 12

25 Adding 6 and 7

Add to find the total. You may use counters or dots.

a $0 + 6 =$ ____	k $1 + 7 =$ ____
b $2 + 6 =$ ____	l $0 + 7 =$ ____
c $1 + 6 =$ ____	m $2 + 7 =$ ____
d $3 + 6 =$ ____	n $4 + 7 =$ ____
e $6 + 6 =$ ____	o $3 + 7 =$ ____
f $5 + 6 =$ ____	p $6 + 7 =$ ____
g $4 + 6 =$ ____	q $5 + 7 =$ ____
h $8 + 6 =$ ____	r $7 + 7 =$ ____
i $9 + 6 =$ ____	s $9 + 7 =$ ____
j $7 + 6 =$ ____	t $8 + 7 =$ ____

26 Enrichment: Adding 8 and 9

Add to find the total. You may use counters or dots.

a 1 + 8 = ____	k 0 + 9 = ____
b 0 + 8 = ____	l 1 + 9 = ____
c 2 + 8 = ____	m 3 + 9 = ____
d 3 + 8 = ____	n 2 + 9 = ____
e 5 + 8 = ____	o 4 + 9 = ____
f 4 + 8 = ____	p 5 + 9 = ____
g 6 + 8 = ____	q 7 + 9 = ____
h 8 + 8 = ____	r 6 + 9 = ____
i 7 + 8 = ____	s 8 + 9 = ____
j 9 + 8 = ____	t 9 + 9 = ____

27 Number words 11–20

11 eleven	14 fourteen	17 seventeen
12 twelve	15 fifteen	18 eighteen
13 thirteen	16 sixteen	19 nineteen
		20 twenty

Write the number to match the word.

a nineteen ____

b fifteen ____

c fourteen ____

d seventeen ____

e sixteen ____

f twelve ____

g twenty ____

h thirteen ____

i eleven ____

j eighteen ____

Review

Write the number to match the word.

a eight ____

b nine ____

c seven ____

d five ____

e three ____

f zero ____

28 Number words 11–20

Write the number word to match the number.

a 15 ________________

b 19 ________________

c 16 ________________

d 13 ________________

e 17 ________________

f 11 ________________

g 12 ________________

h 20 ________________

i 18 ________________

j 14 ________________

Review

Write the number or the number word.

a 9 ________________

b eleven ________________

c 0 ________________

d sixteen ________________

e 12 ________________

f seven ________________

g 18 ________________

h fifteen ________________

i 1 ________________

j ten ________________

29 Tens and ones

Circle 10. Write how many tens and ones.

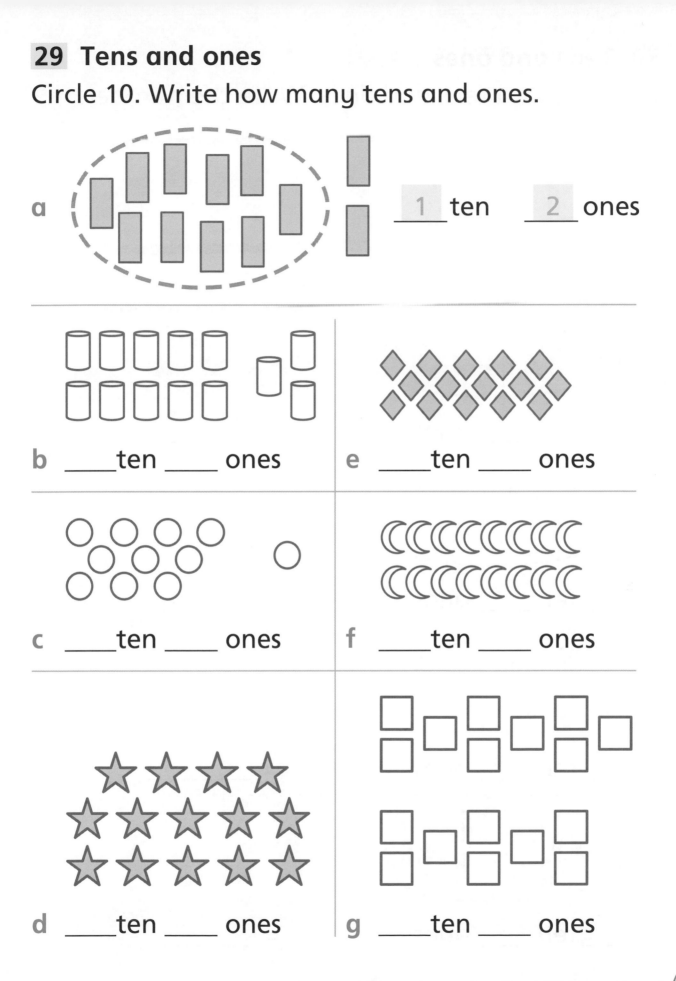

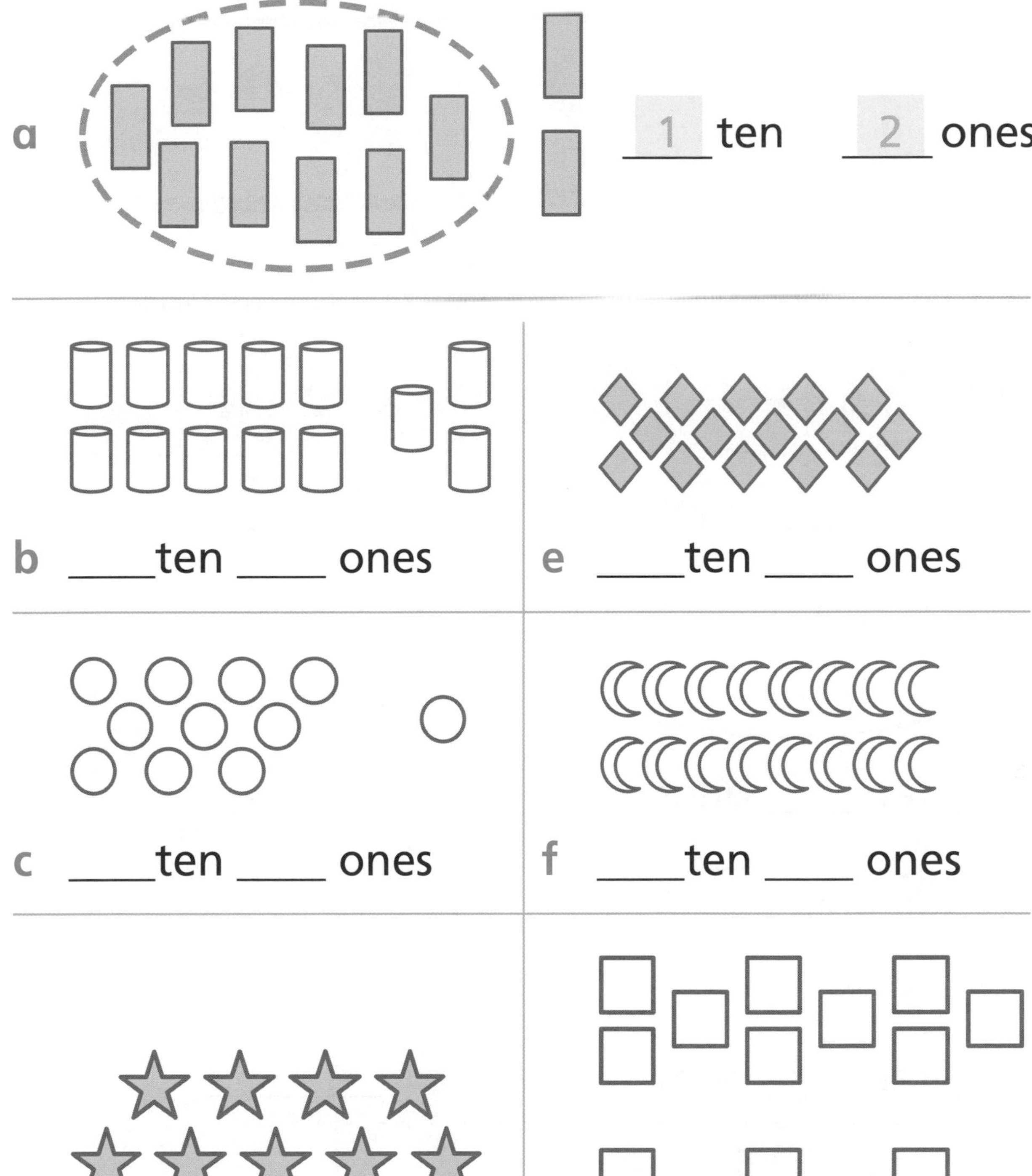

a 1 ten 2 ones

b ____ten ____ ones

e ____ten ____ ones

c ____ten ____ ones

f ____ten ____ ones

d ____ten ____ ones

g ____ten ____ ones

30 Tens and ones

Separate into tens and ones. Write the number.

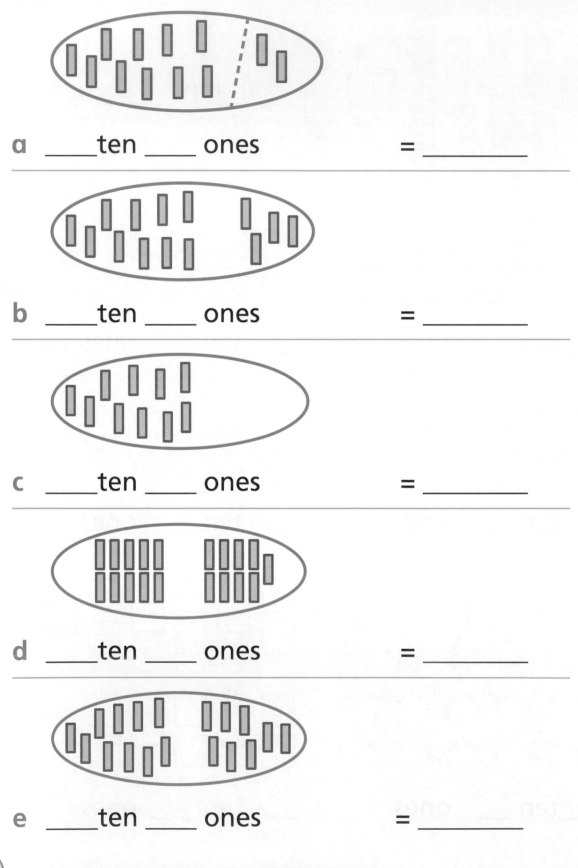

a ____ten ____ ones = ________

b ____ten ____ ones = ________

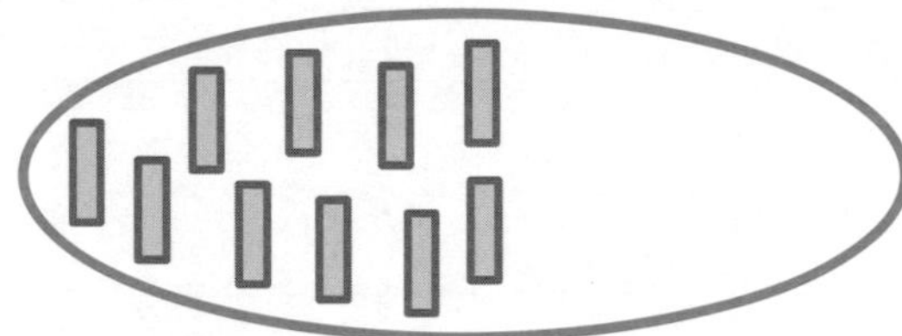

c ____ten ____ ones = ________

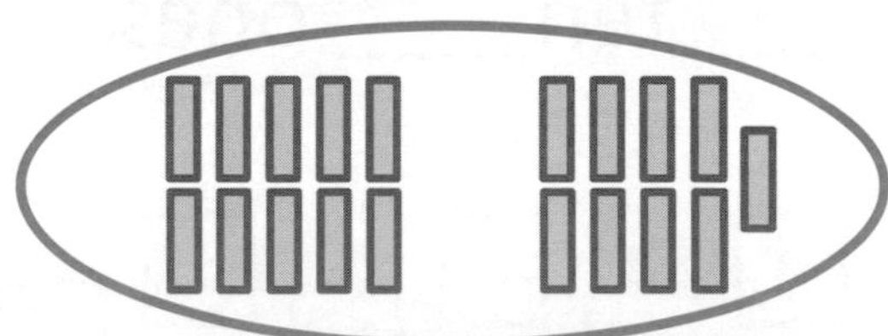

d ____ten ____ ones = ________

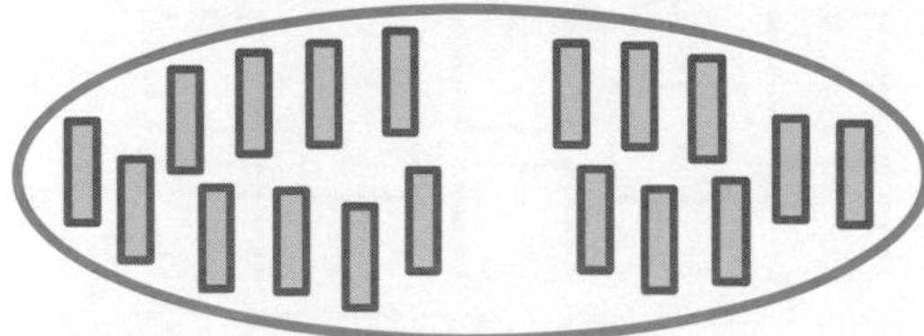

e ____ten ____ ones = ________

31 Tens and ones

Circle ten. Write the tens and ones. Write the number.

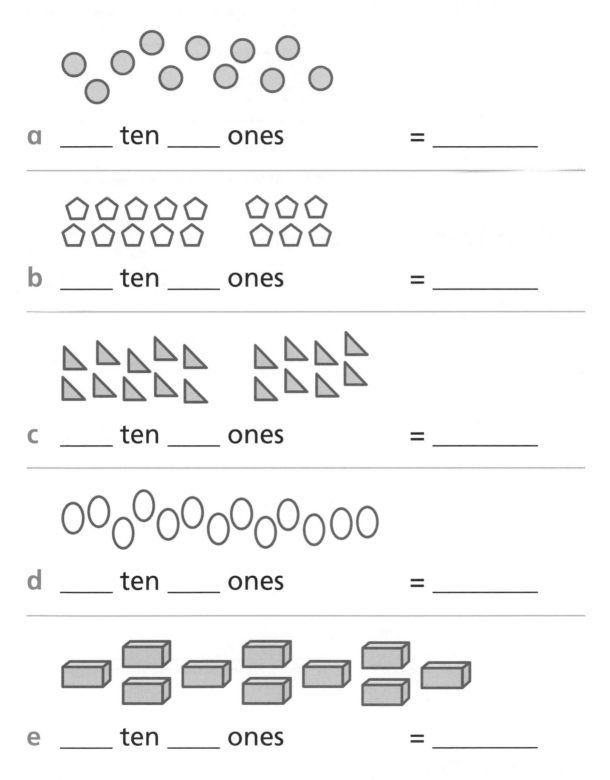

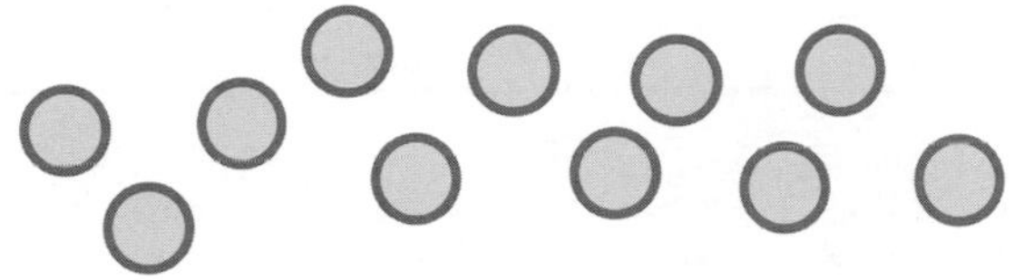

a ____ ten ____ ones = ________

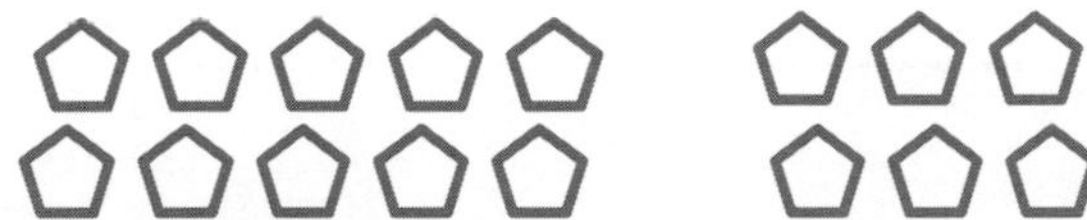

b ____ ten ____ ones = ________

c ____ ten ____ ones = ________

d ____ ten ____ ones = ________

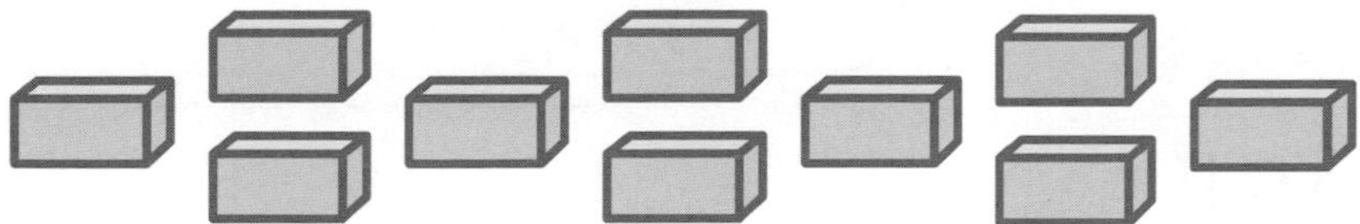

e ____ ten ____ ones = ________

Unit 3: Patterns and sequences

1 One less and one more

Write the number and draw the set.

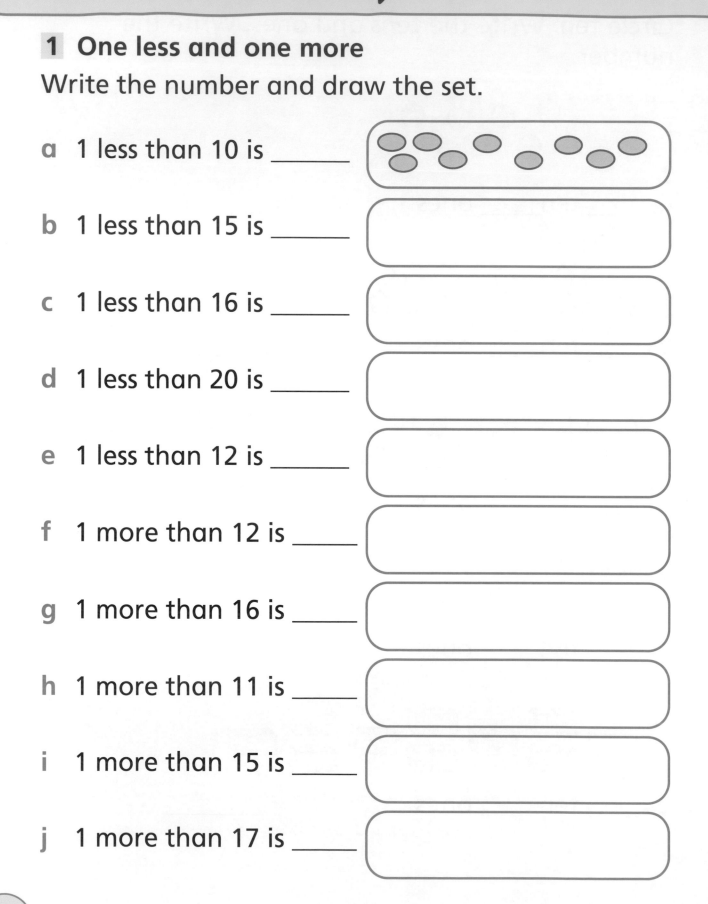

a 1 less than 10 is ______

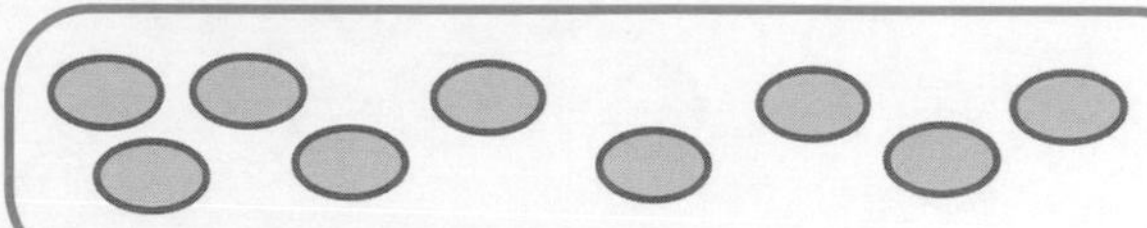

b 1 less than 15 is ______

c 1 less than 16 is ______

d 1 less than 20 is ______

e 1 less than 12 is ______

f 1 more than 12 is ______

g 1 more than 16 is ______

h 1 more than 11 is ______

i 1 more than 15 is ______

j 1 more than 17 is ______

2 Numbers in sequence

Write the missing numbers.

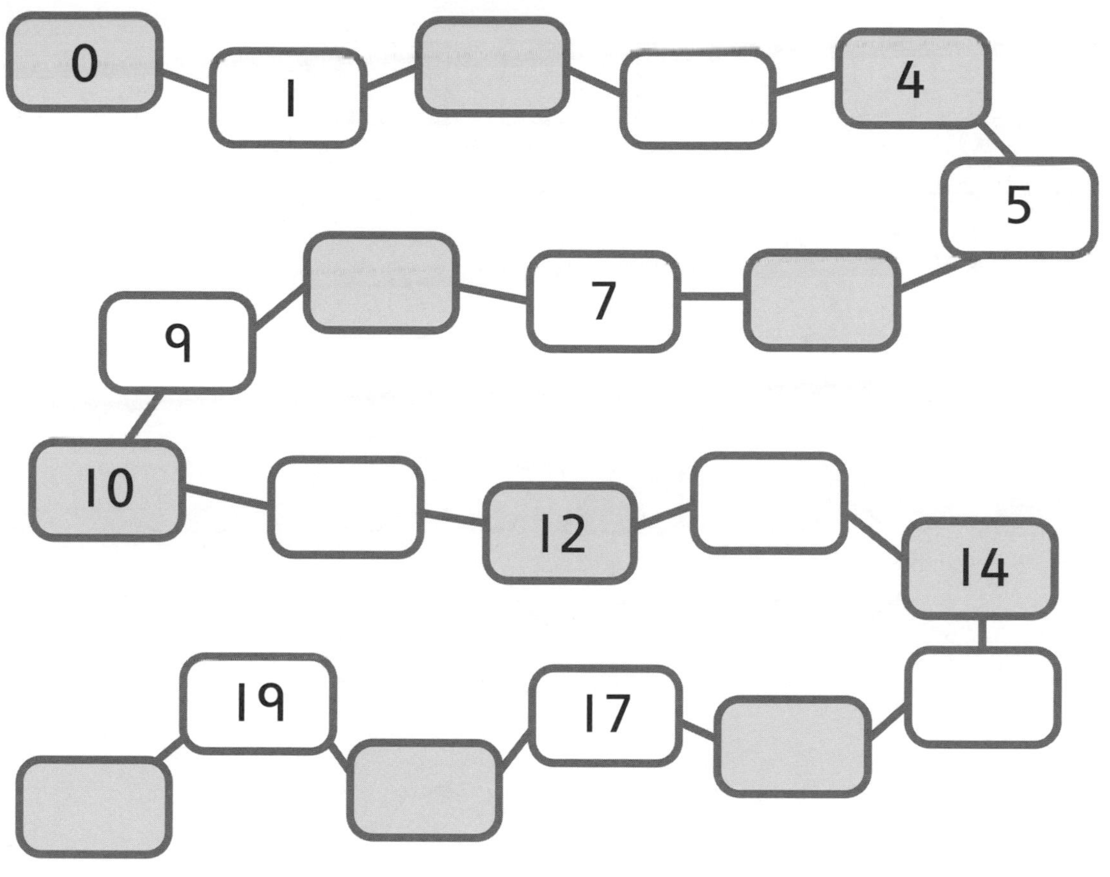

Write all the counting numbers in order from 1 to 20.

1 _____ _____ _____ _____

_____ _____ _____ _____ _____

_____ _____ _____ _____ _____

_____ _____ _____ _____ _____

3 Completing patterns

Draw the next shapes in each pattern.

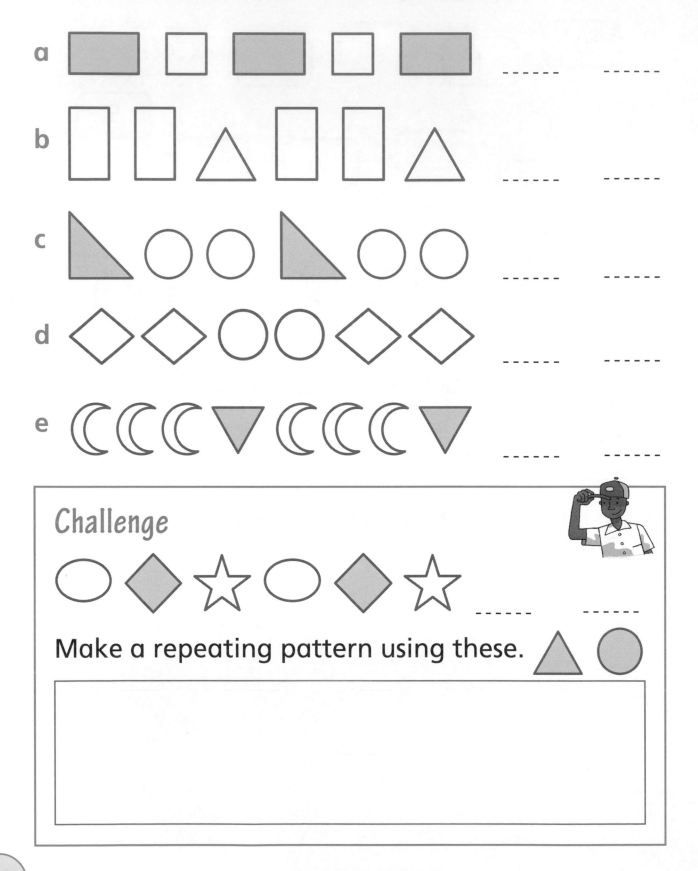

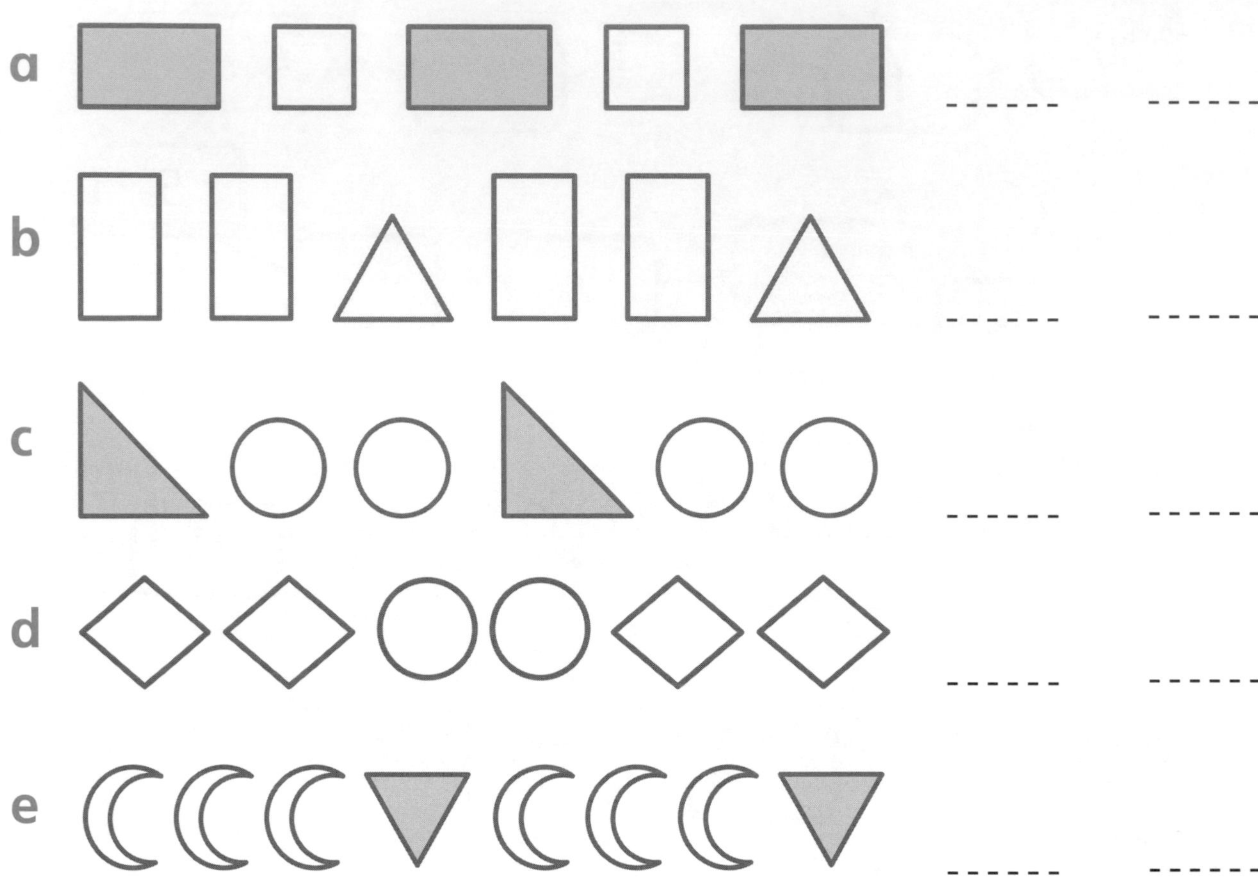

Challenge

Make a repeating pattern using these.

4 Completing patterns

Draw the missing shapes to complete these patterns.

a ....

b ....

c ....

d ....

e ....

Challenge

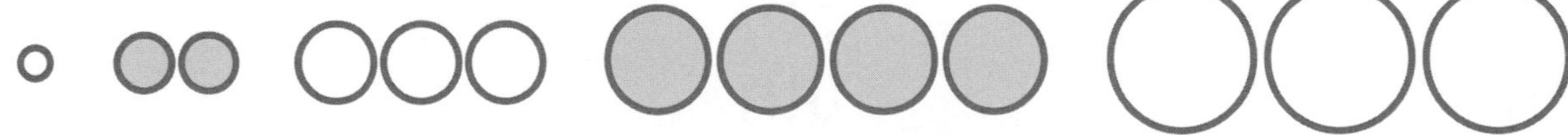

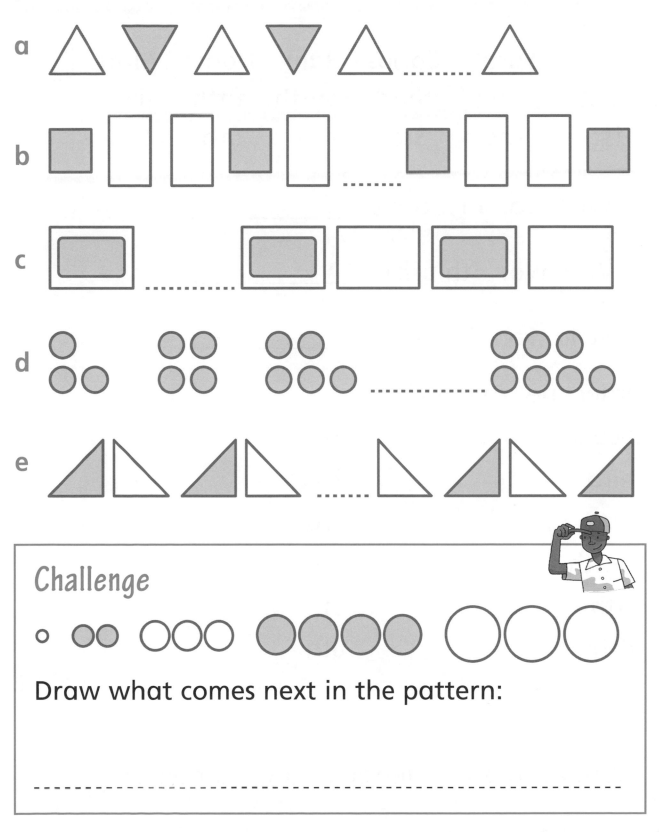

Draw what comes next in the pattern:

----

5 Ordinal numbers

Ana	Sarah	Carlos	Rani	Dante	Matt
first	second	third	fourth	fifth	sixth
1st	2nd	3rd	4th	5th	6th

a Who won first prize? ____________

b Who won 4th prize? ____________

c Who won third? ____________

Draw lines to match.

second	1st
third	2nd
first	3rd
fourth	4th
sixth	5th
fifth	6th

Challenge

What is the fifth letter of your surname? ____

6 Ordinal numbers

Draw five balloons in the box.

a Colour the second balloon blue.

b Colour the 3rd balloon green.

c Draw a long string on the fifth balloon.

d Draw six bananas in the box above.

e Circle the 4th banana.

f Cross out the sixth banana.

Challenge

  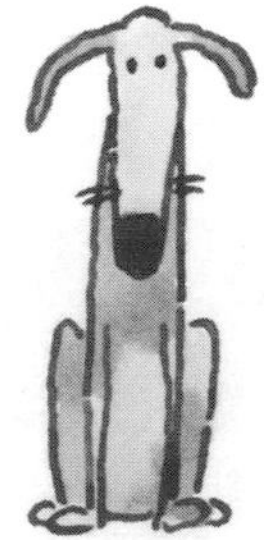  

The dog on the left won 1st place in the dog show. Draw a first place ribbon on it.

7 Comparing numbers: more than

Count the shapes. Use **>** to show **is more than**.

Larger number

Circle the group with more. Draw the symbol > with the open mouth by the group that **is more than**.

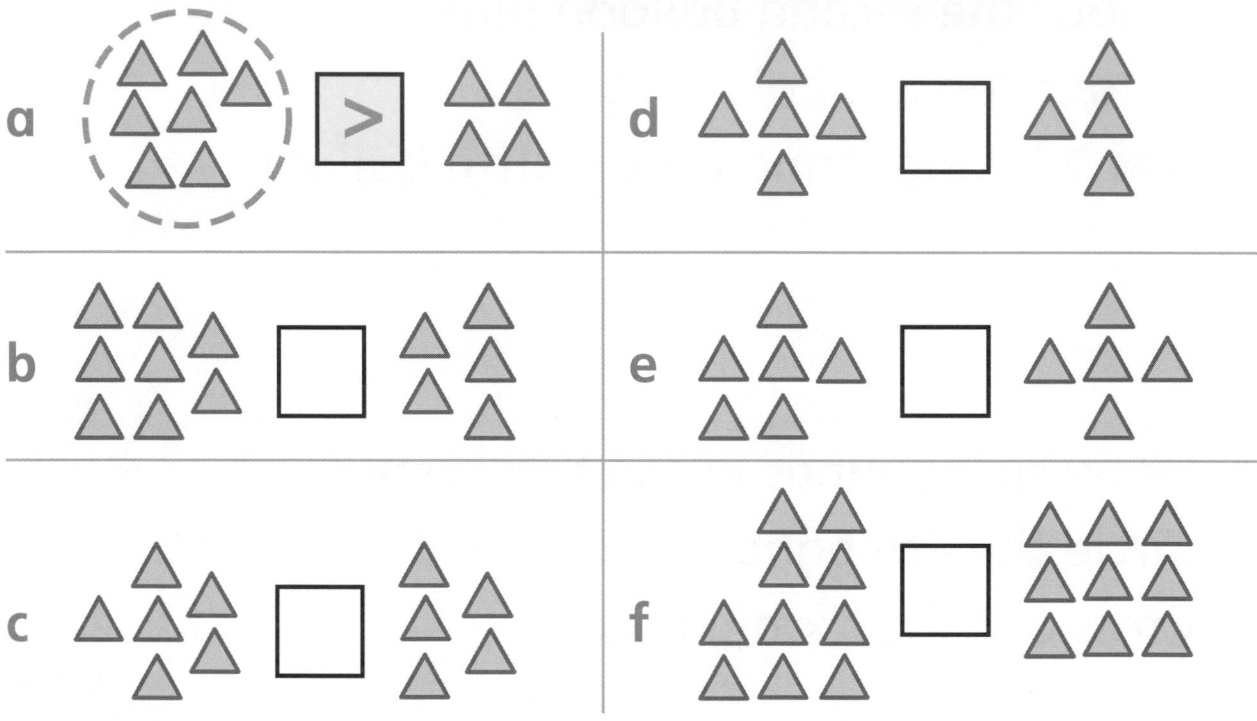

Count and write how many shapes. Put the symbol > with the open part by the group that **is more than**.

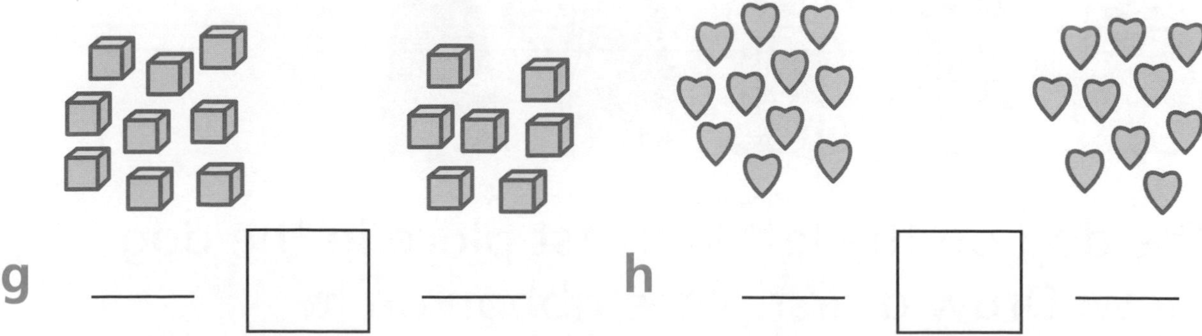

8 Comparing numbers: less than

Count the shapes. Use **<** to show **is less than**.

smaller number

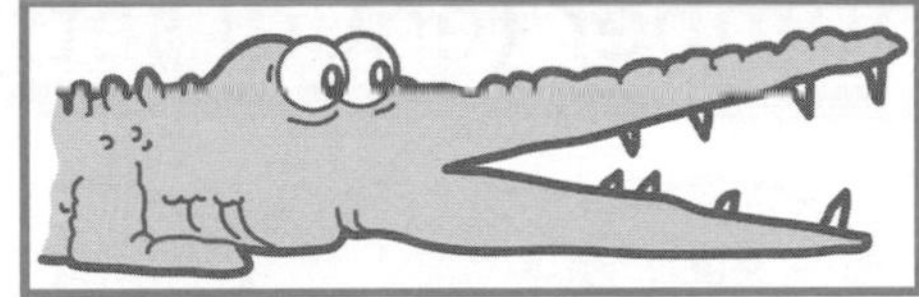

Circle the group that is less. Draw the symbol < with the point by the group that has fewer shapes.

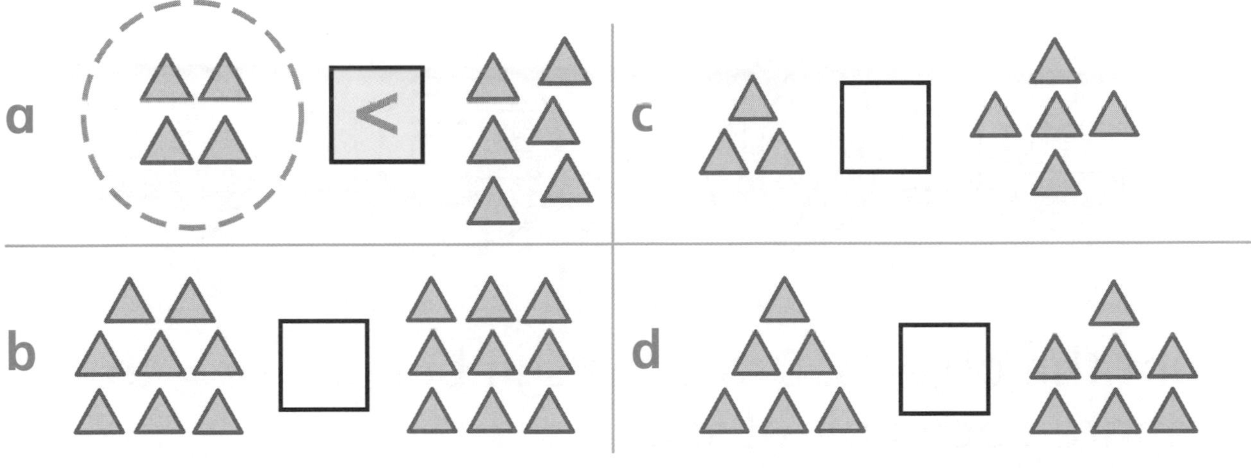

Count. Put the symbol < with the point by the group that **is less than**. Then write the numbers and the symbol.

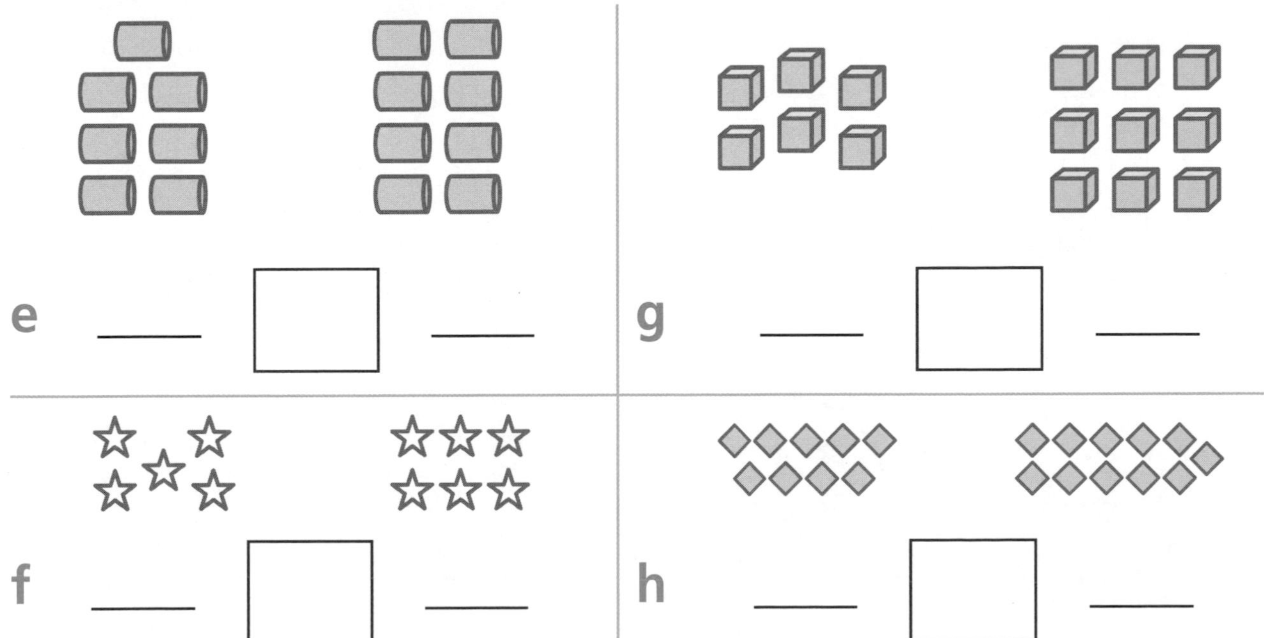

9 Comparing numbers: the same as

Count. Use **=** to show **is the same as** when the sets have the same number (equal sets).

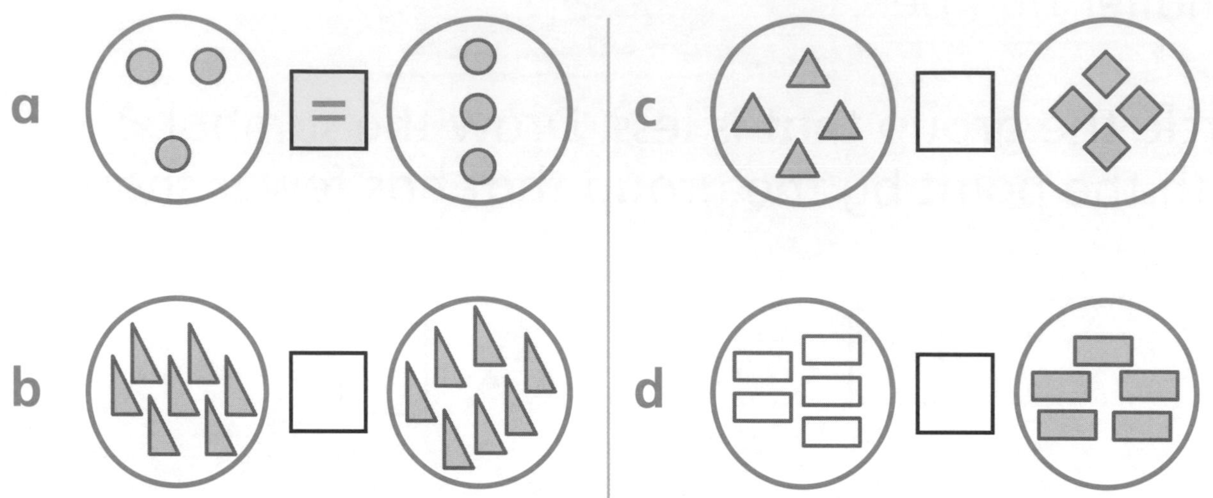

Count the objects. Draw the symbol <, = or > to compare each pair of sets.

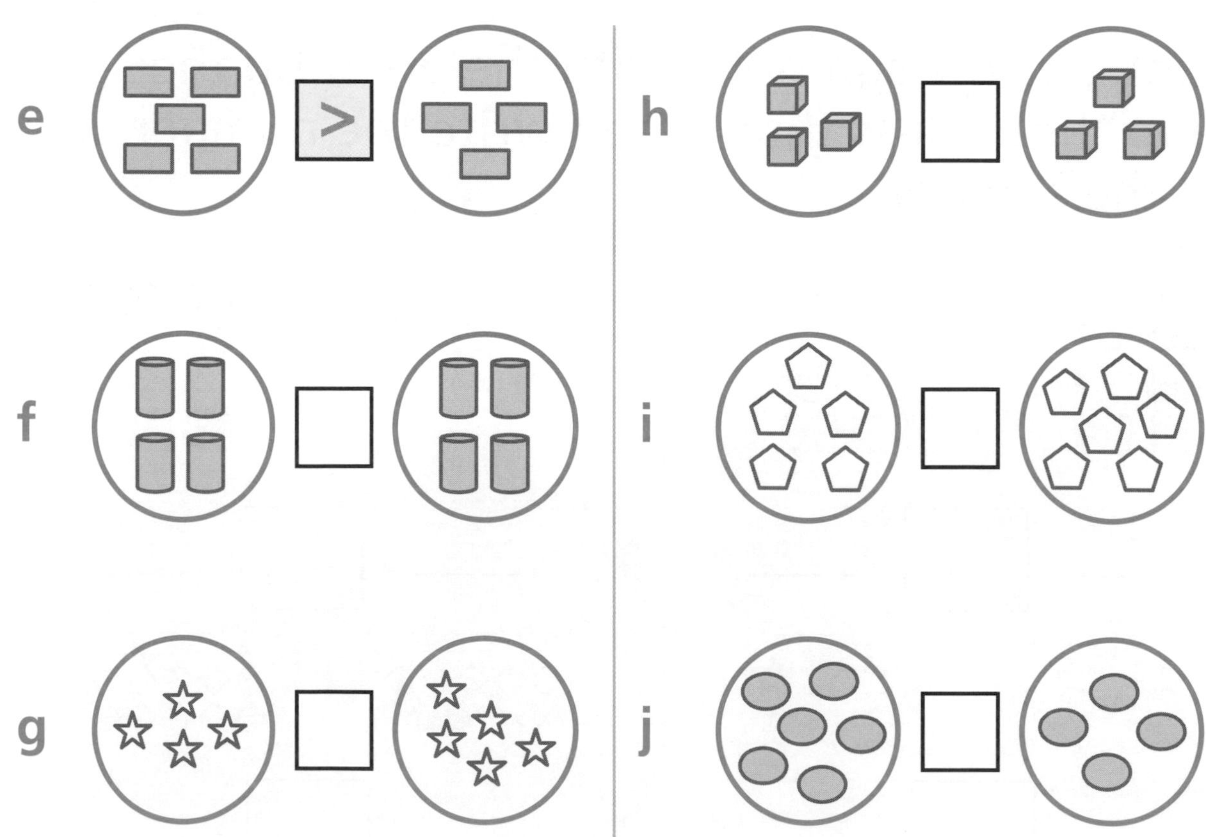

1 Count the objects.

Draw the symbol <, = or > to compare each pair of sets.

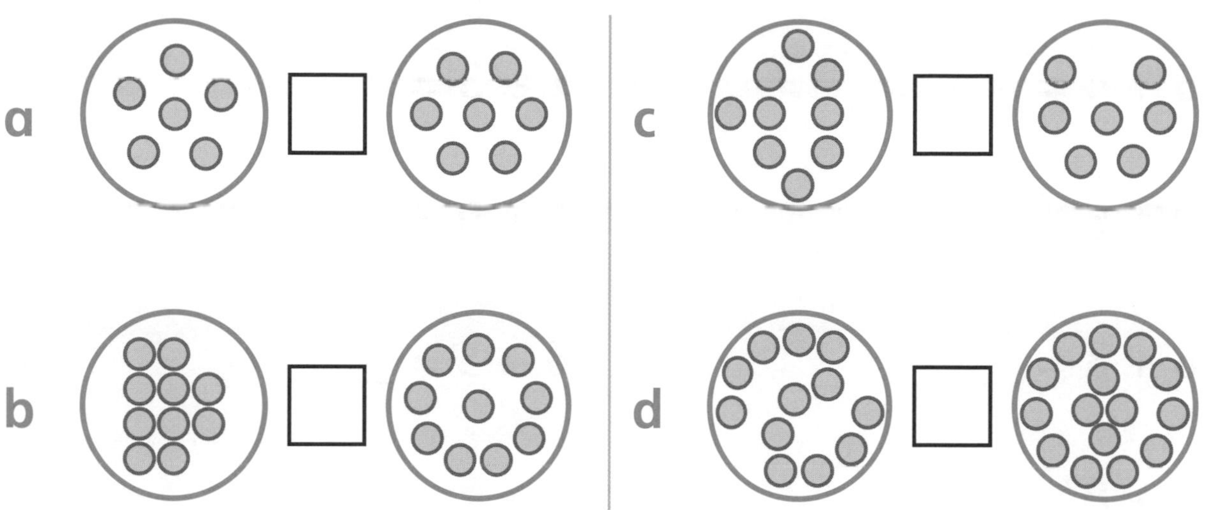

2 Look at the letters in the word: **wonderful**.

e What letter is 4th? ____

f What letter is sixth? ____

3

g What 2 shapes come next?

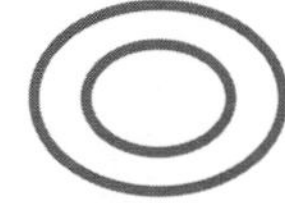

______ ______

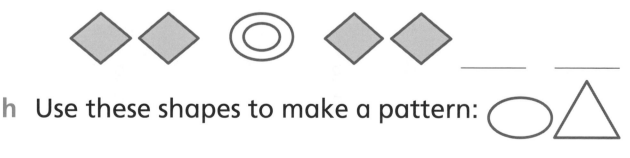

h Use these shapes to make a pattern: 

Unit 4: More number and operations

1 Review and practice

a $5 + 2 =$ ____

b $3 + 4 =$ ____

c $0 + 6 =$ ____

d $8 + 3 =$ ____

e $4 + 8 =$ ____

f $6 + 6 =$ ____

g $7 + 3 =$ ____

h $1 + 9 =$ ____

i $6 + 5 =$ ____

j $9 + 2 =$ ____

k $\begin{array}{r} 12 \\ +\ 0 \\ \hline \end{array}$ ____

l $\begin{array}{r} 8 \\ +\ 6 \\ \hline \end{array}$ ____

m $\begin{array}{r} 5 \\ +\ 8 \\ \hline \end{array}$ ____

n $\begin{array}{r} 5 \\ +\ 3 \\ \hline \end{array}$ ____

o $\begin{array}{r} 7 \\ +\ 2 \\ \hline \end{array}$ ____

p $\begin{array}{r} 3 \\ +\ 9 \\ \hline \end{array}$ ____

q $\begin{array}{r} 11 \\ +\ 1 \\ \hline \end{array}$ ____

r $\begin{array}{r} 4 \\ +\ 7 \\ \hline \end{array}$ ____

s $\begin{array}{r} 9 \\ +\ 5 \\ \hline \end{array}$ ____

2 Review and practice

Add.

a $4 + 3 =$ ____

$3 + 4 =$ ____

$$\begin{array}{r} 4 \\ +\ 3 \\ \hline \\ \hline \end{array} \qquad \begin{array}{r} 3 \\ +\ 4 \\ \hline \\ \hline \end{array}$$

b $2 + 9 =$ ____

$9 + 2 =$ ____

$$\begin{array}{r} 2 \\ +\ 9 \\ \hline \\ \hline \end{array} \qquad \begin{array}{r} 9 \\ +\ 2 \\ \hline \\ \hline \end{array}$$

c $5 + 7 =$ ____

$7 + 5 =$ ____

$$\begin{array}{r} 5 \\ +\ 7 \\ \hline \\ \hline \end{array} \qquad \begin{array}{r} 7 \\ +\ 5 \\ \hline \\ \hline \end{array}$$

d $6 + 8 =$ ____

$8 + 6 =$ ____

$$\begin{array}{r} 6 \\ +\ 8 \\ \hline \\ \hline \end{array} \qquad \begin{array}{r} 8 \\ +\ 6 \\ \hline \\ \hline \end{array}$$

Challenge

a Look at each set of sums shown above.
What do you notice? ________________________

____

b $12 + 12 =$ ________________

3 Addition word problems

Add. Then write the number sentence.

a 9 birds are on the line.

4 birds are on the poles.

There are ____ birds in all.

Number sentence ______________

---

b There are 6 tall trees. 5 trees are short.

Draw the trees in the box.

Altogether, there are ____ trees.

Number sentence ______________

---

c There are 7 kites over the sea.

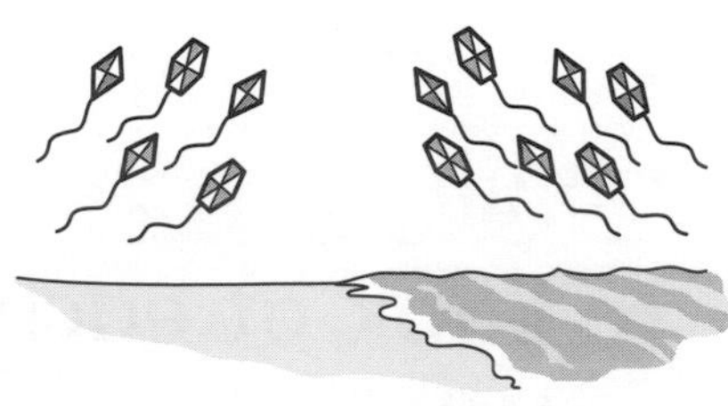

There are 5 kites over the land.

There are ____ kites altogether.

Number sentence ______________

4 Using number lines to add

Find the first number on the number line. Count on 5 jumps.

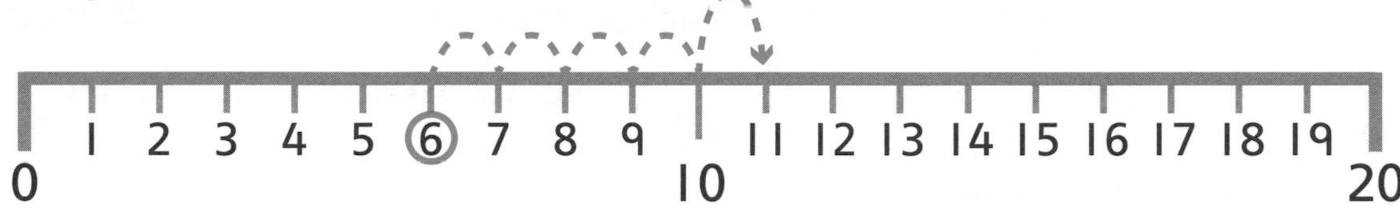

a Show 6 + 5 = ☐

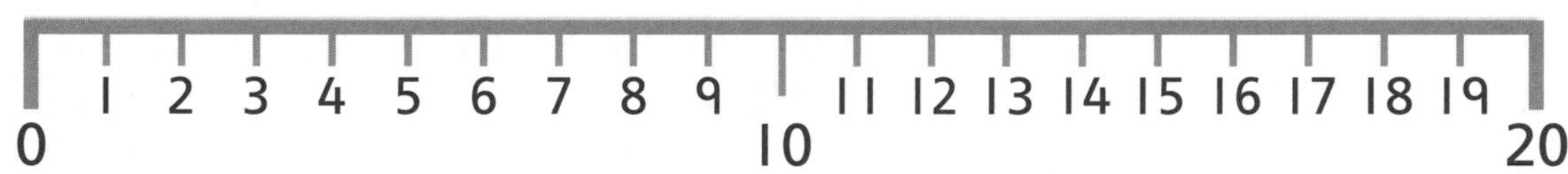

b Show 7 + 4 = ☐

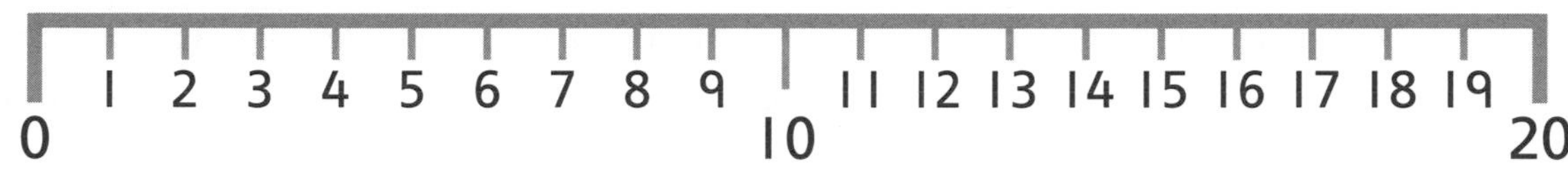

c Show 14 + 3 = ☐

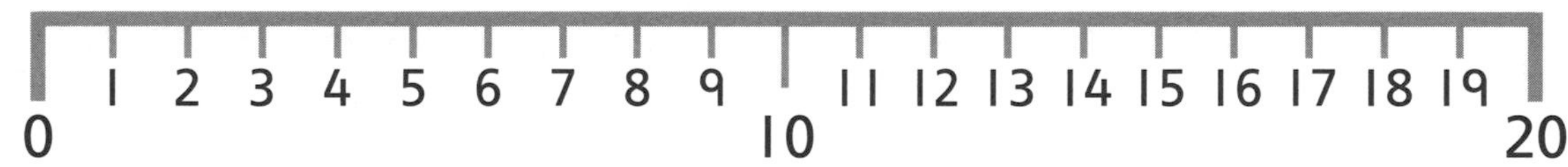

d Show 5 + 7 = ☐

0 1 2 3 4 5 6 7 8 9 10 11 12 13 14 15 16 17 18 19 20

e Show 10 + 5 = ☐

5 Using number lines to add

Use the number line. Add.

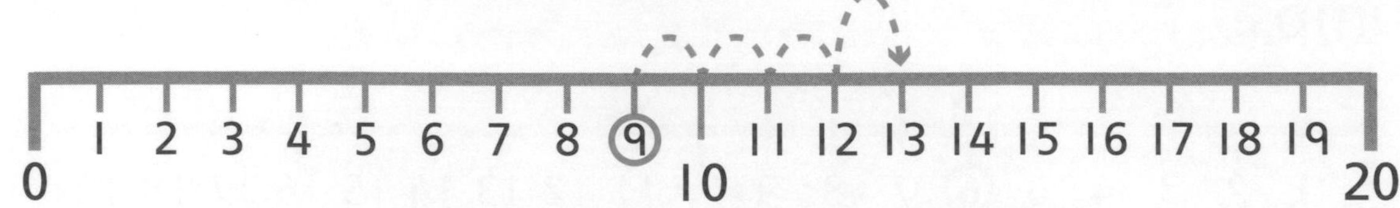

a Show 9 + 4 = ☐

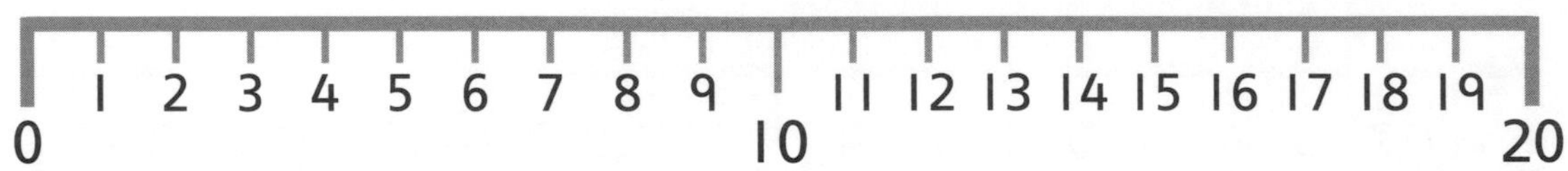

b Show 4 + 6 = ☐

---

c Show 7 + 7 = ☐

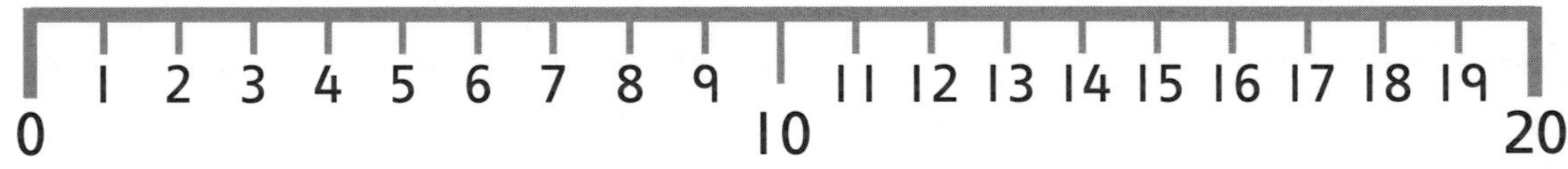

d Show 10 + 8 = ☐

---

e Show 12 + 3 = ☐

6 Using number lines to add

Use the number line. Add.

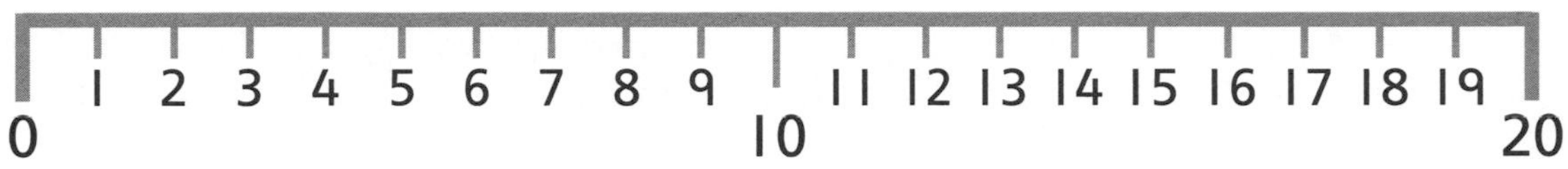

a Show 6 + 7 = ☐

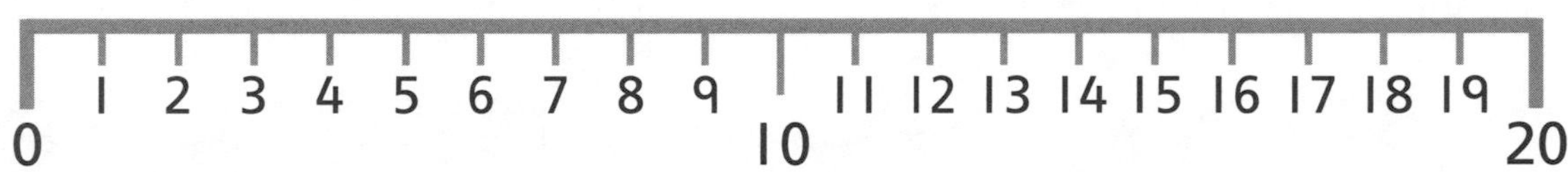

b Show 3 + 8 = ☐

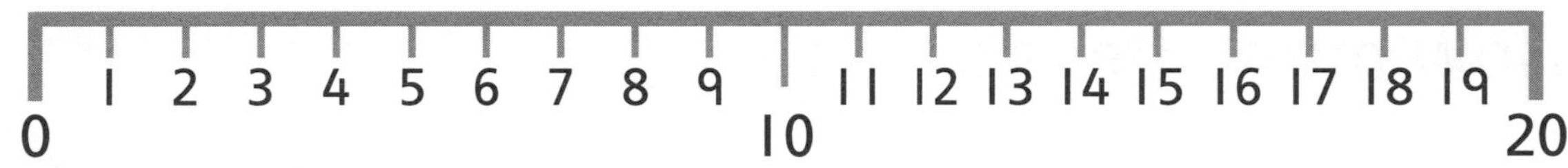

c Show 13 + 7 = ☐

0 1 2 3 4 5 6 7 8 9 10 11 12 13 14 15 16 17 18 19 20

d Show 12 + 6 = ☐

0 1 2 3 4 5 6 7 8 9 10 11 12 13 14 15 16 17 18 19 20

e Show 14 + 4 = ☐

7 Getting ready to subtract

a Match each pencil to a ruler.

How many are left? ____

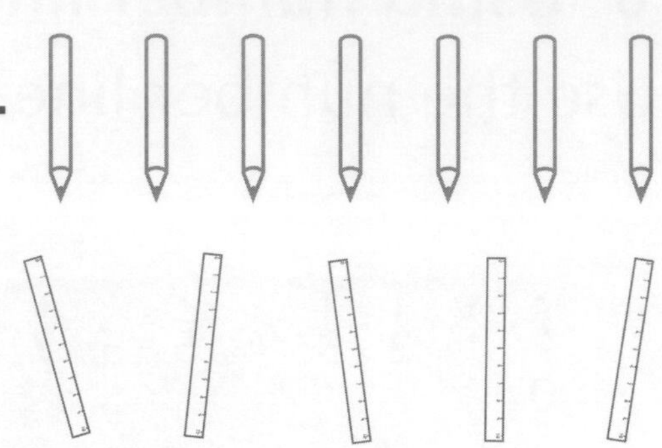

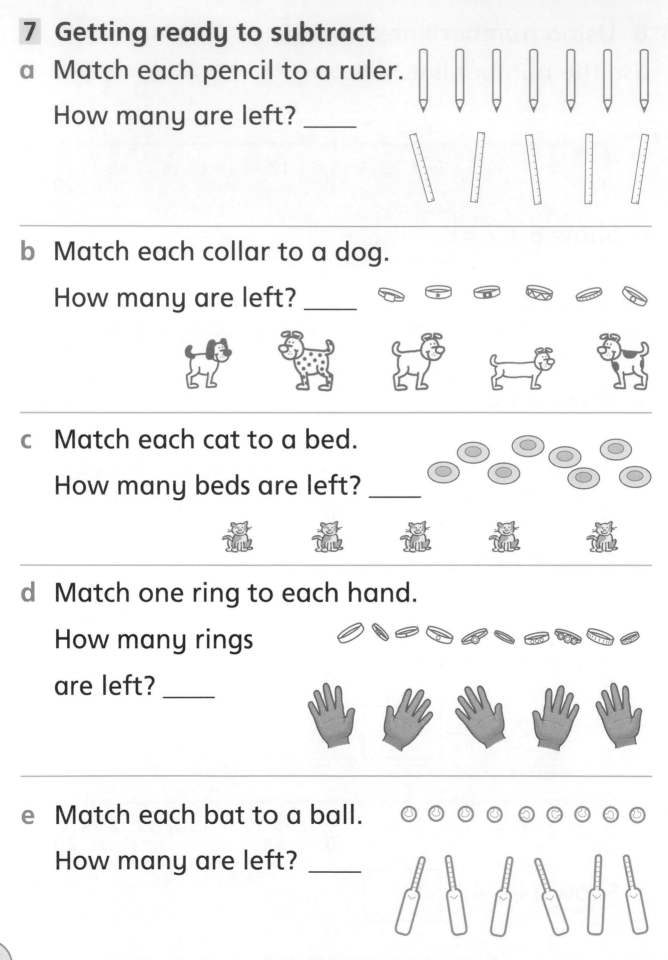

b Match each collar to a dog.

How many are left? ____

c Match each cat to a bed.

How many beds are left? ____

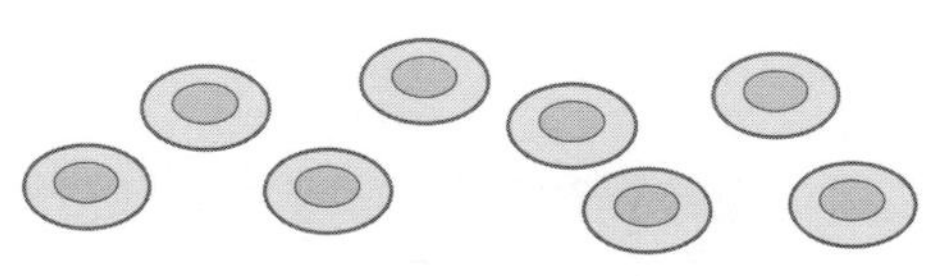

d Match one ring to each hand.

How many rings are left? ____

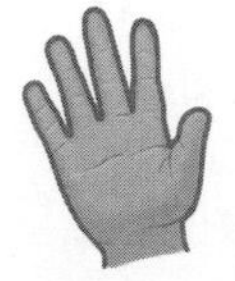
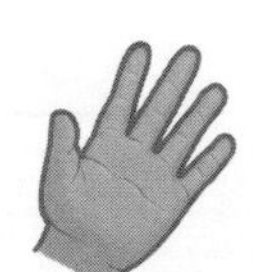
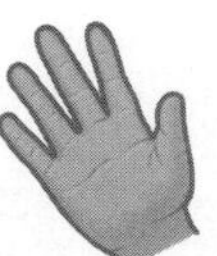
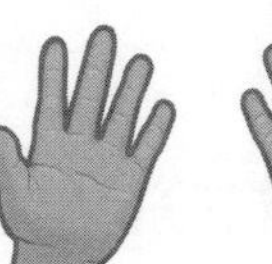
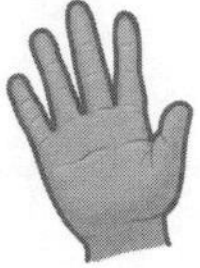

e Match each bat to a ball.

How many are left? ____

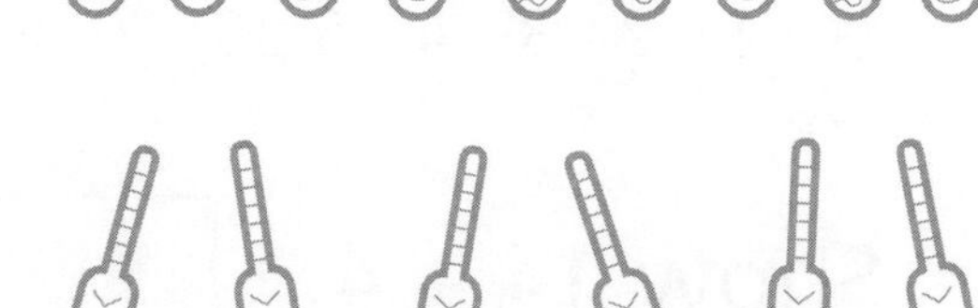

8 Subtraction with objects

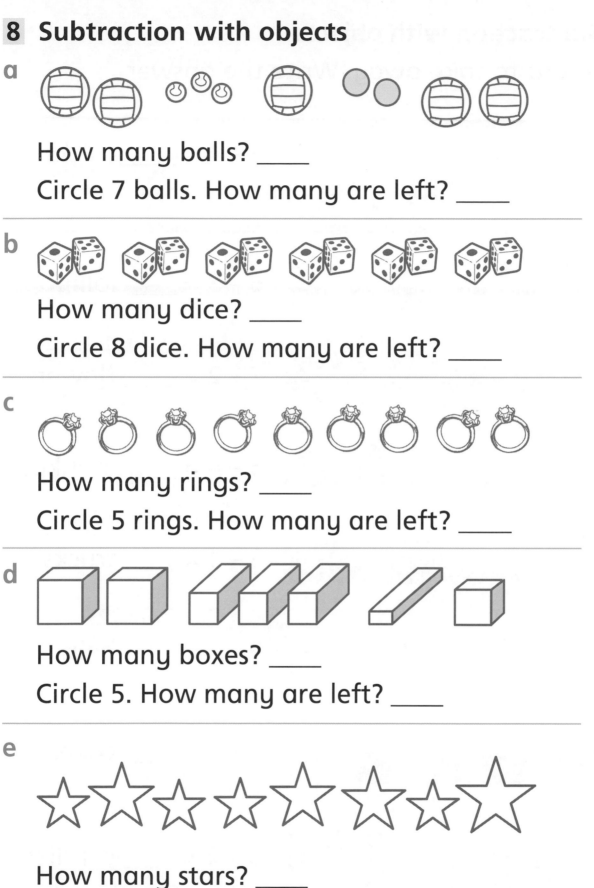

a

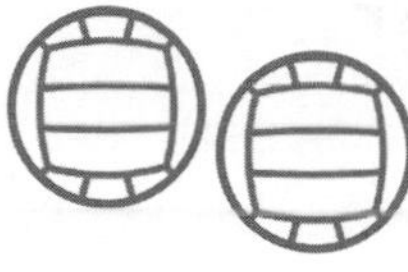  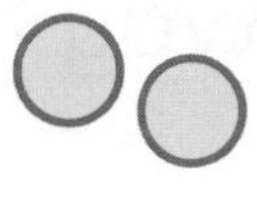 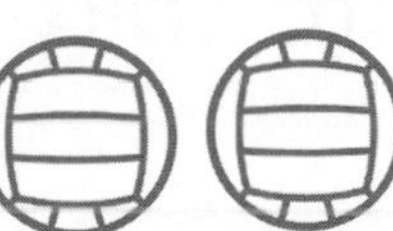

How many balls? ____

Circle 7 balls. How many are left? ____

b

How many dice? ____

Circle 8 dice. How many are left? ____

c

    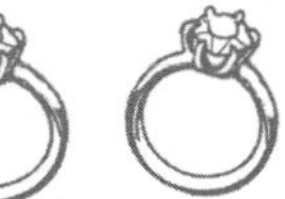   

How many rings? ____

Circle 5 rings. How many are left? ____

d

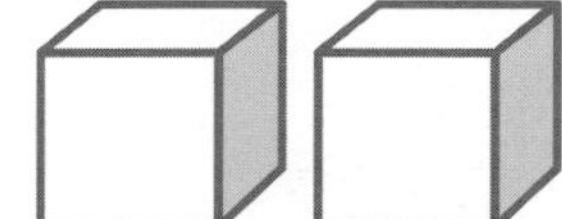  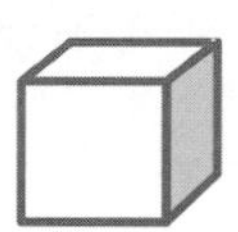

How many boxes? ____

Circle 5. How many are left? ____

e

How many stars? ____

Circle 3 stars. How many are left? ____

9 Subtraction with objects

Cross out to take away. Write the answer.

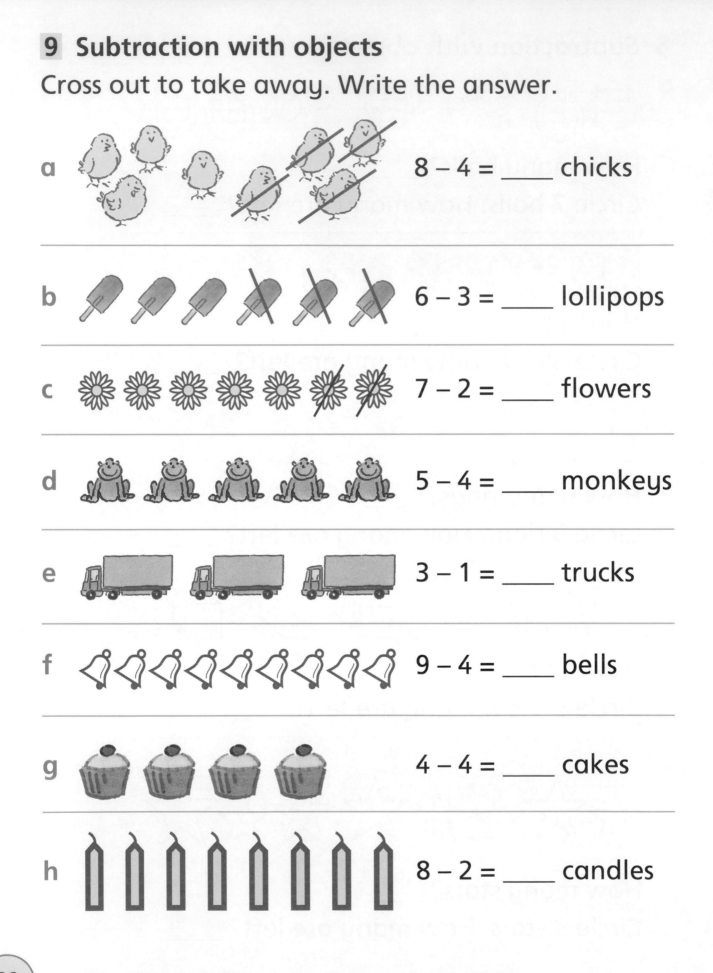

a  8 – 4 = ____ chicks

b  6 – 3 = ____ lollipops

c  7 – 2 = ____ flowers

d    5 – 4 = ____ monkeys

e    3 – 1 = ____ trucks

f  9 – 4 = ____ bells

g  4 – 4 = ____ cakes

h 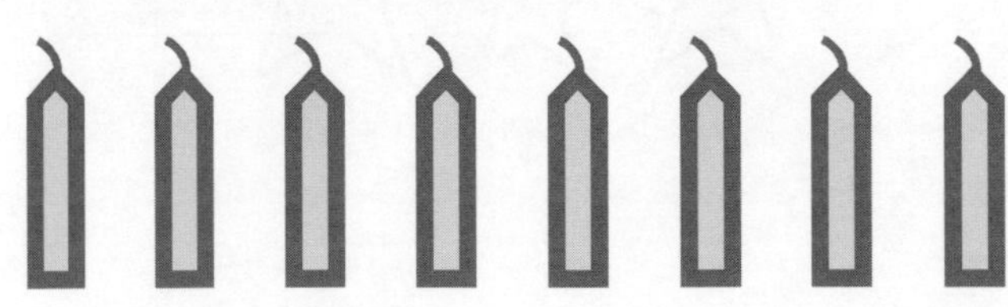 8 – 2 = ____ candles

10 Subtracting 0 or 1

Subtract to find the answers.

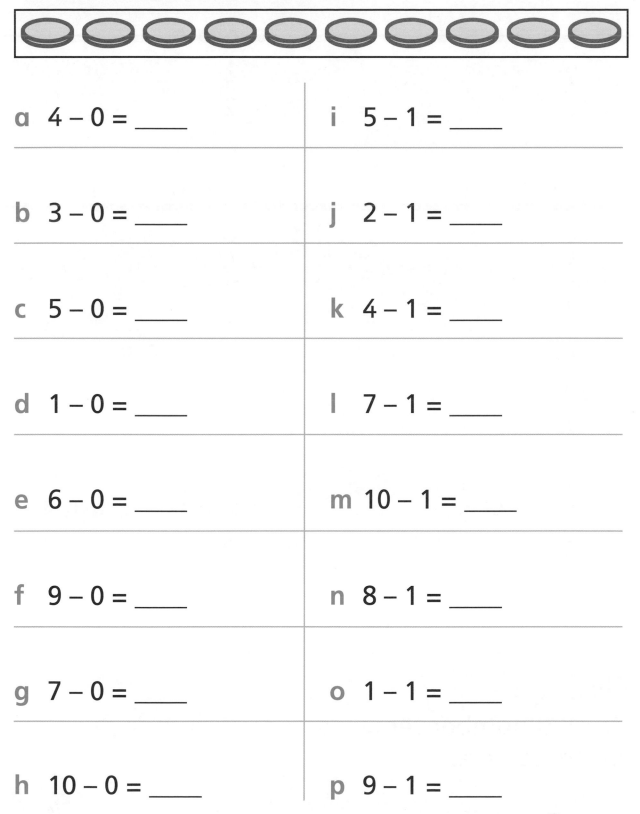

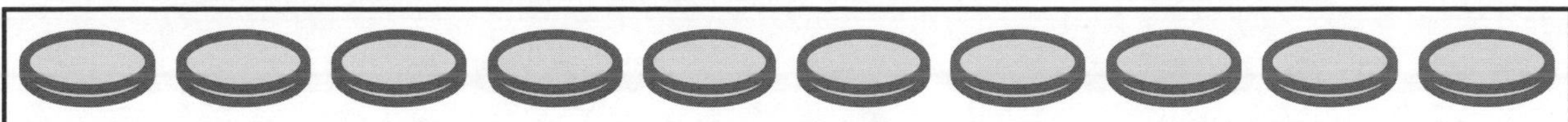

a 4 – 0 = ____	i 5 – 1 = ____
b 3 – 0 = ____	j 2 – 1 = ____
c 5 – 0 = ____	k 4 – 1 = ____
d 1 – 0 = ____	l 7 – 1 = ____
e 6 – 0 = ____	m 10 – 1 = ____
f 9 – 0 = ____	n 8 – 1 = ____
g 7 – 0 = ____	o 1 – 1 = ____
h 10 – 0 = ____	p 9 – 1 = ____

11 Subtracting using dots

Count. Cross out the dots you take away.

a
```
  7
- 3
___

___
```

b
```
  6
- 1
___

___
```

c
```
 10
- 3
___

___
```

d
```
  5
- 5
___

___
```

e
```
  4
- 2
___

___
```

f
```
  8
- 5
___

___
```

g
```
  6
- 4
___

___
```

h
```
  9
- 5
___

___
```

Challenge

Write a number sentence for these dots.

____ – ____ = ____

12 Subtraction word problems

a 6 balloons are in the air.

3 go away.

____ balloons are left.

Number sentence

____

b 7 vans are parked.

1 drives away.

____ vans are left.

Number sentence ____________________

c 5 children are playing.

2 go home.

____ children are left.

Number sentence

____

d 8 cakes are on the plate.

4 are eaten.

____ cakes are left.

Number sentence ____________________

13 Subtraction using number lines

Draw a line and count back. Subtract.

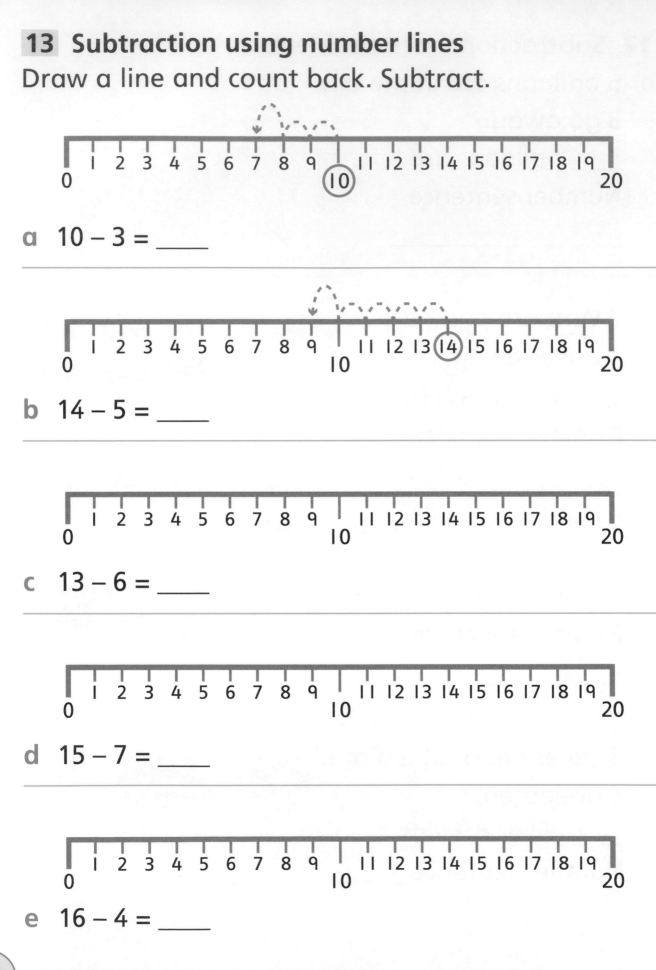

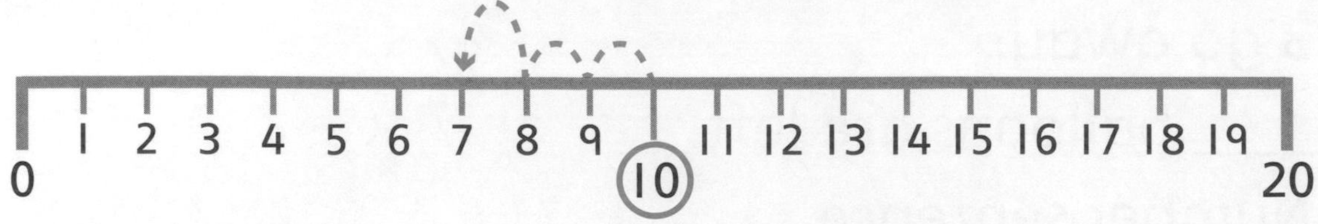

a 10 – 3 = ____

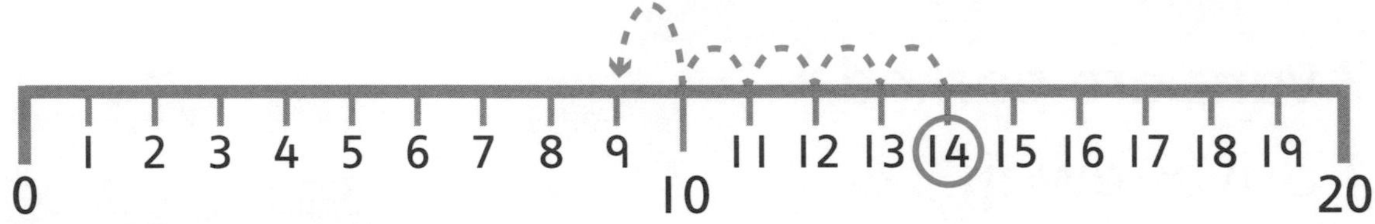

b 14 – 5 = ____

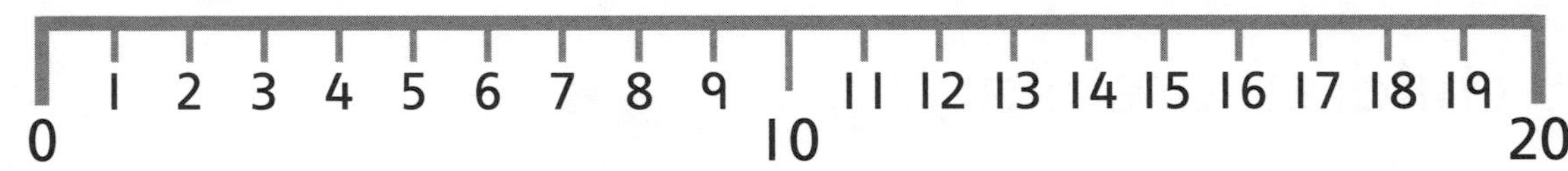

c 13 – 6 = ____

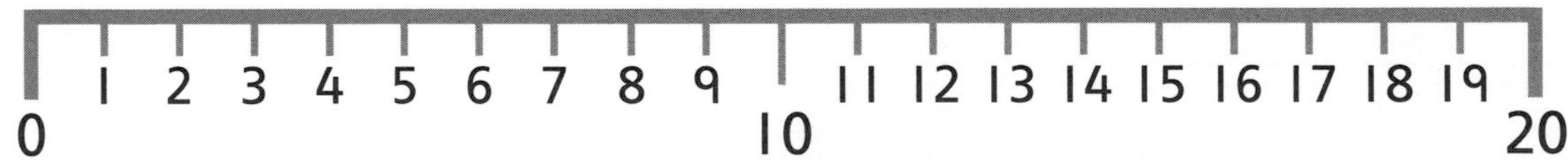

d 15 – 7 = ____

0 1 2 3 4 5 6 7 8 9 10 11 12 13 14 15 16 17 18 19 20

e 16 – 4 = ____

14 Subtraction using number lines

Draw a line and count back. Subtract.

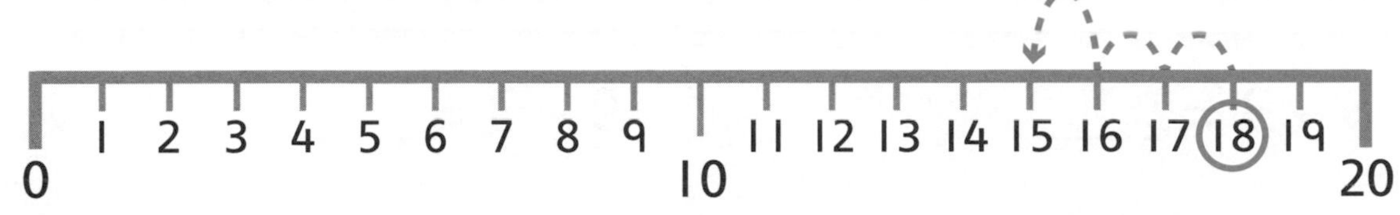

a 18 – 3 = ____

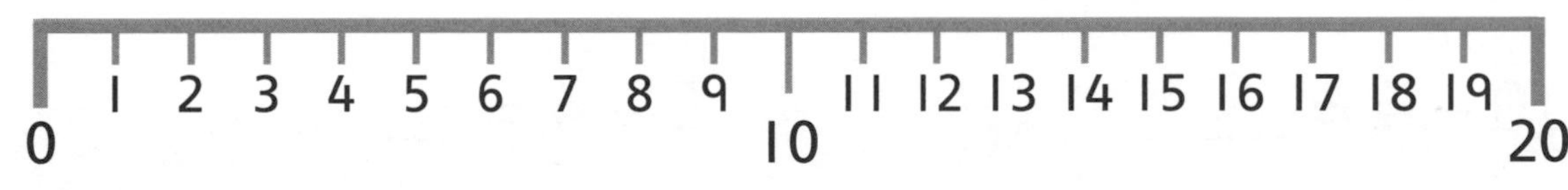

b 13 – 8 = ____

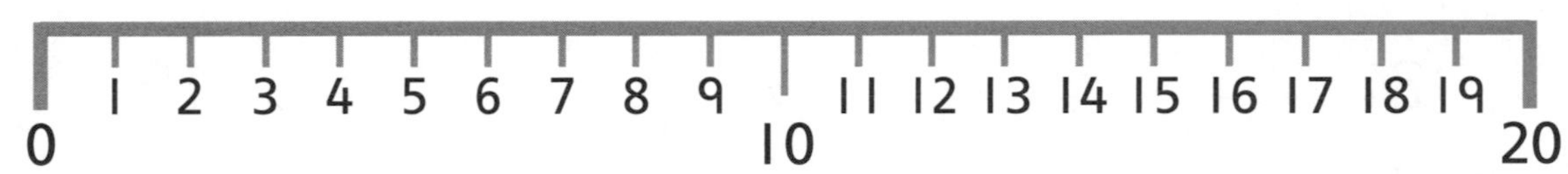

c 17 – 6 = ____

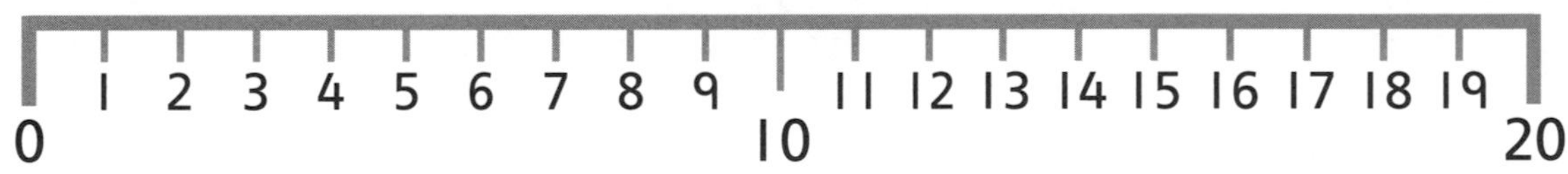

d 12 – 9 = ____

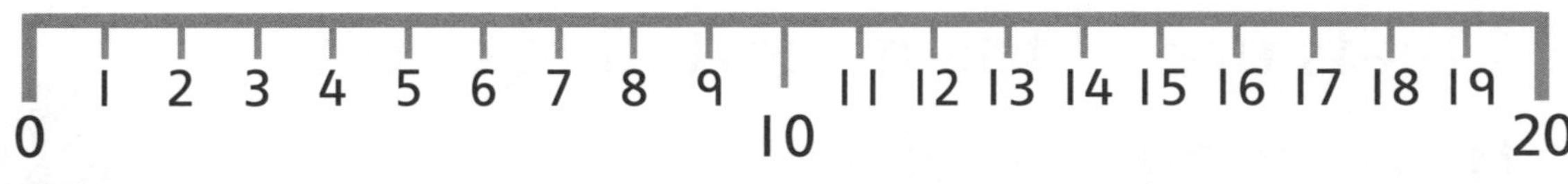

e 19 – 5 = ____

15 Subtraction practice

Subtract to find the answers. You may draw dots or use your ruler as a number line, if you wish.

a $8 - 3 =$ ____

b $7 - 5 =$ ____

c $11 - 10 =$ ____

d $10 - 4 =$ ____

e $6 - 6 =$ ____

f $9 - 3 =$ ____

g $12 - 10 =$ ____

h $8 - 6 =$ ____

i $5 - 4 =$ ____

j $10 - 6 =$ ____

Review

a $\begin{array}{r} 8 \\ - \ 5 \\ \hline \end{array}$

b $\begin{array}{r} 12 \\ - \ 7 \\ \hline \end{array}$

c $\begin{array}{r} 11 \\ - \ 8 \\ \hline \end{array}$

d $\begin{array}{r} 9 \\ - \ 2 \\ \hline \end{array}$

e $\begin{array}{r} 8 \\ - \ 7 \\ \hline \end{array}$

f $\begin{array}{r} 10 \\ - \ 9 \\ \hline \end{array}$

g $\begin{array}{r} 10 \\ - \ 0 \\ \hline \end{array}$

h $\begin{array}{r} 11 \\ - \ 5 \\ \hline \end{array}$

i $\begin{array}{r} 12 \\ - 11 \\ \hline \end{array}$

j 11 jets are at the airport. 6 take off.
How many are left? ____________
Number sentence ____________

16 Subtraction: missing numbers

Draw dots for the first number. Circle the dots in the answer. Fill in the missing numbers.

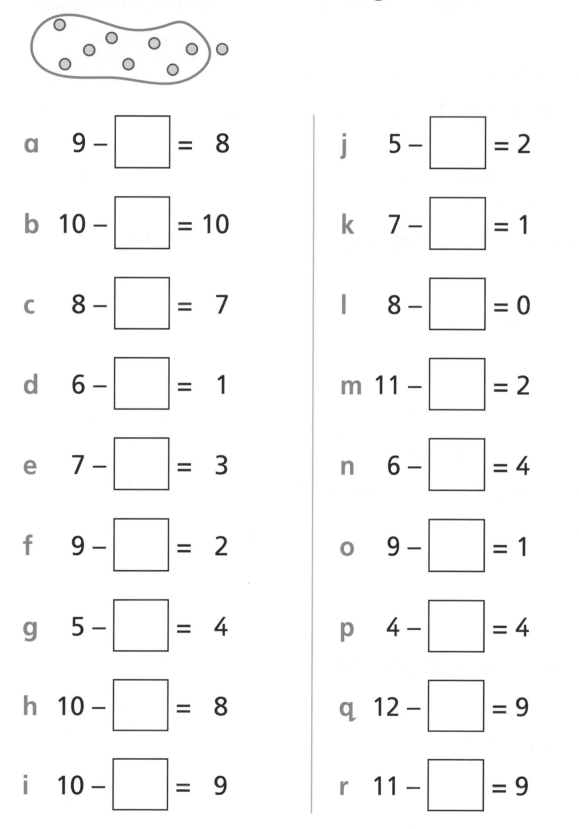

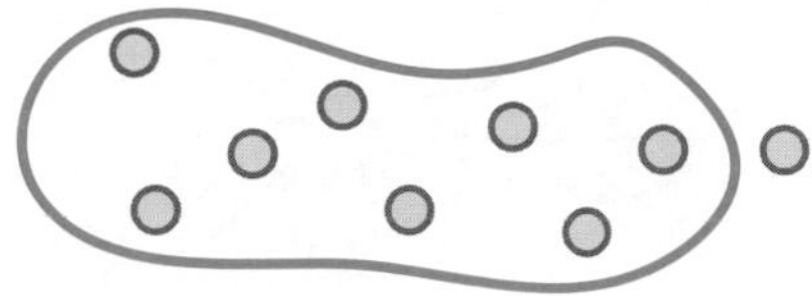

a 9 – ☐ = 8

b 10 – ☐ = 10

c 8 – ☐ = 7

d 6 – ☐ = 1

e 7 – ☐ = 3

f 9 – ☐ = 2

g 5 – ☐ = 4

h 10 – ☐ = 8

i 10 – ☐ = 9

j 5 – ☐ = 2

k 7 – ☐ = 1

l 8 – ☐ = 0

m 11 – ☐ = 2

n 6 – ☐ = 4

o 9 – ☐ = 1

p 4 – ☐ = 4

q 12 – ☐ = 9

r 11 – ☐ = 9

17 Subtraction word problems

Write the number sentence. Subtract.

a There are 13 bananas.
Rita ate 2 bananas.
How many bananas are left?
Number sentence ______________

b 15 marbles are in the bag.
Manuel lost 4 marbles.
How many marbles are left?
Number sentence ______________

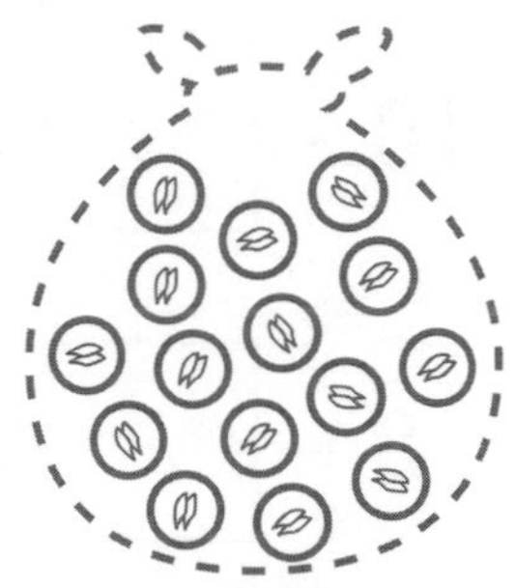

c There are 18 pencils in the jar.
6 pencils are taken.
How many pencils are left?
Number sentence ______________

d Jake has 17 counters.
He gave away 5 counters.
How many counters are left?
Number sentence ______________

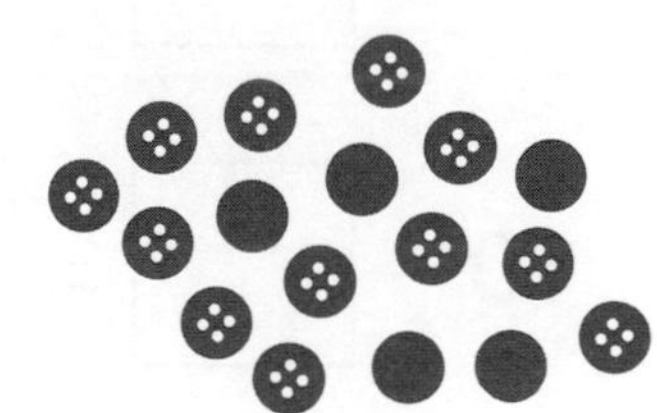

18 Families of number facts

Complete. Use the fact family boxes to help you.

2	1	3

a 2 + 1 = 3

1 + ___ = 3

3 – 2 = ___

3 – ___ = 2

2	6	8

c 2 + ___ = 8

___ + 2 = 8

8 – 6 = ___

___ – 2 = 6

4	2	6

b 4 + ___ = 6

2 + ___ = 6

6 – 2 = ___

___ – 4 = 2

5	6	11

d ___ + 6 = 11

6 + ___ = 11

11 – ___ = 6

___ – ___ = 5

3	7	10

e

$$\begin{array}{r} \bigcirc \\ +\ 7 \\ \hline 10 \end{array} \qquad \begin{array}{r} 7 \\ +\ 3 \\ \hline \_\_\_ \end{array}$$

$$\begin{array}{r} 10 \\ -\ \bigcirc \\ \hline 3 \end{array} \qquad \begin{array}{r} 10 \\ -\ \bigcirc \\ \hline 7 \end{array}$$

8	2	10

f

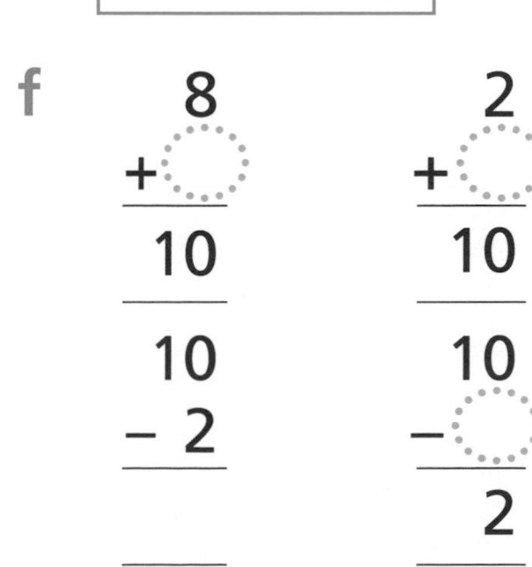

19 Families of number facts

Complete. Use the fact family boxes to help you.

4 8 12

a $4 + 8 =$ ___

___ $+ 4 = 12$

$12 -$ ___ $= 8$

$12 -$ ___ $= 4$

3 4 7

c $3 +$ ___ $= 7$

___ $+ 3 = 7$

$7 -$ ___ $= 3$

___ $- 3 = 4$

4 5 9

b $4 +$ ___ $= 9$

$5 + 4 =$ ___

$9 - 5 =$ ___

___ $- 4 = 5$

1 4 5

d ___ $+ 1 = 5$

___ $+ 4 = 5$

$5 -$ ___ $= 4$

___ $-$ ___ $= 1$

5 7 12

e

$$\begin{array}{r} 5 \\ + \bigcirc \\ \hline 12 \\ \hline \end{array} \qquad \begin{array}{r} 7 \\ +\ 5 \\ \hline \\ \hline \end{array}$$

$$\begin{array}{r} 12 \\ - \bigcirc \\ \hline 5 \\ \hline \end{array} \qquad \begin{array}{r} \bigcirc \\ -\ 5 \\ \hline 7 \\ \hline \end{array}$$

3 8 11

f

$$\begin{array}{r} 8 \\ + \bigcirc \\ \hline \\ \hline \end{array} \qquad \begin{array}{r} 3 \\ + \bigcirc \\ \hline 11 \\ \hline \end{array}$$

$$\begin{array}{r} 11 \\ - \bigcirc \\ \hline 8 \\ \hline \end{array} \qquad \begin{array}{r} 11 \\ - \bigcirc \\ \hline 3 \\ \hline \end{array}$$

Unit 5: Money

1 Coins

Find the total money.

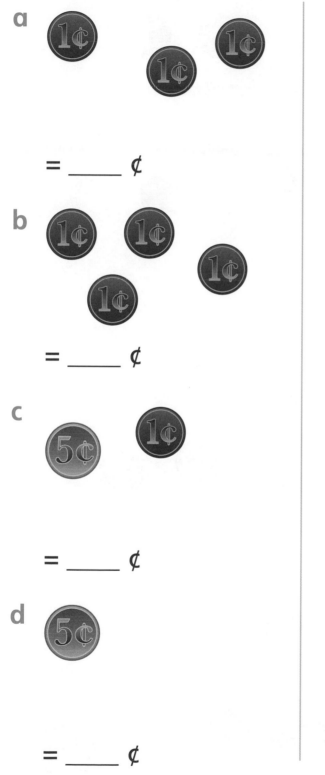

a

= _____ ¢

b

= _____ ¢

c

= _____ ¢

d

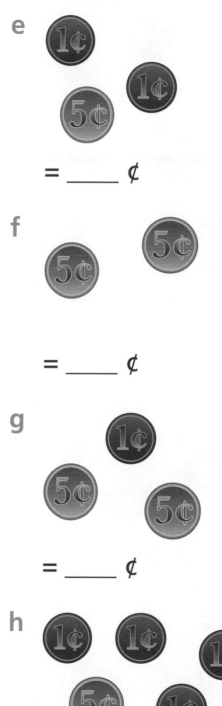

= _____ ¢

e

= _____ ¢

f

= _____ ¢

g

= _____ ¢

h

= _____ ¢

2 Coins

Find the total money.

a

= _____ ¢

b

= _____ ¢

c

= _____ ¢

d

= _____ ¢

e

= _____ ¢

f

= _____ ¢

g

= _____ ¢

h

= _____ ¢

Challenge

= _____ ¢

= _____ ¢

3 Notes

Find the total dollars.

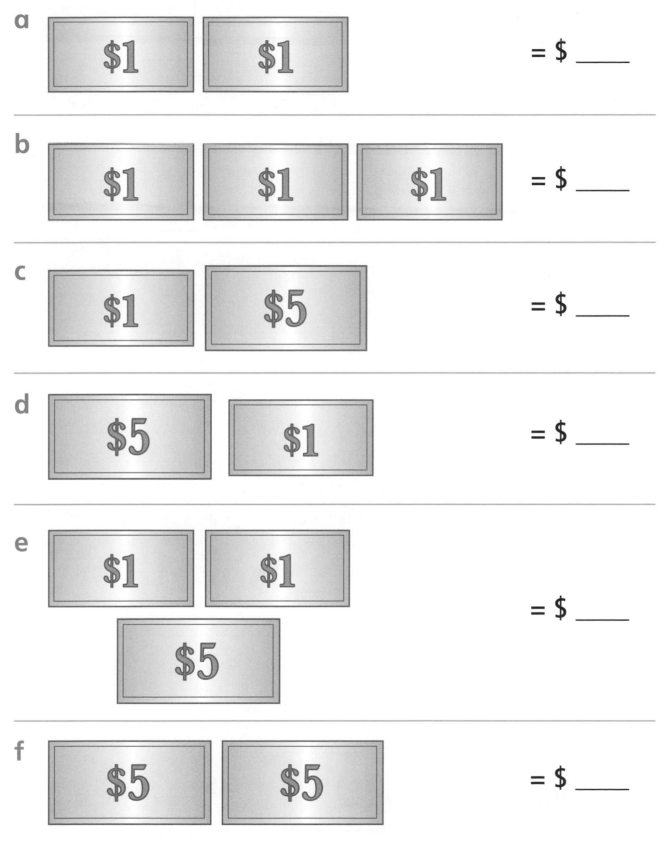

a

$1

= $ ____

b

$1 $1

= $ ____

c

$5

= $ ____

d

$1

= $ ____

e

$1

= $ ____

f

$5

= $ ____

4 Notes

Find the total dollars.

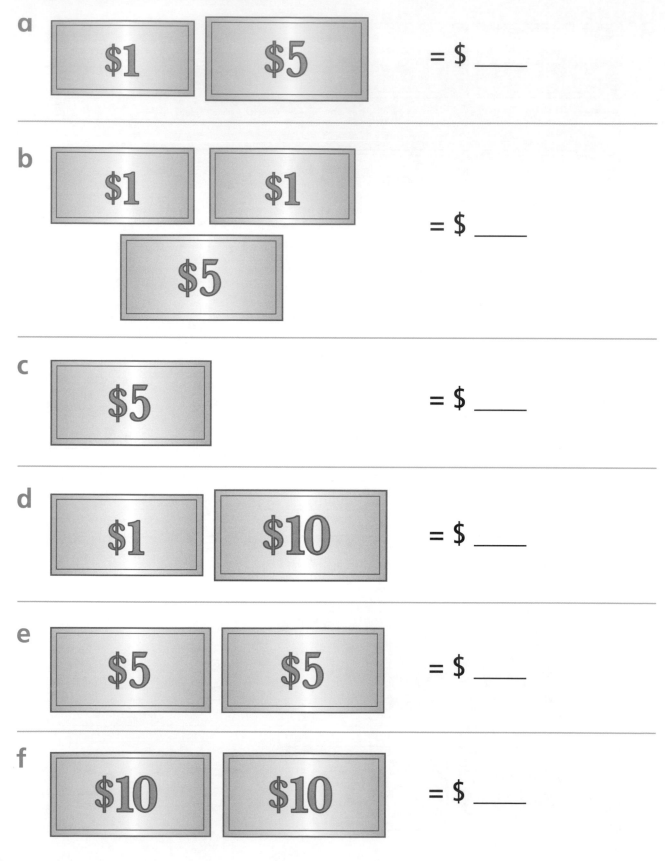

a

$5

= $ ____

b

$1

$5

= $ ____

c

$5

= $ ____

d

$10

= $ ____

e

$5

= $ ____

f

$10

$10

= $ ____

5 Using coins to buy

Use these coins. 

a Draw the coins you need to buy.

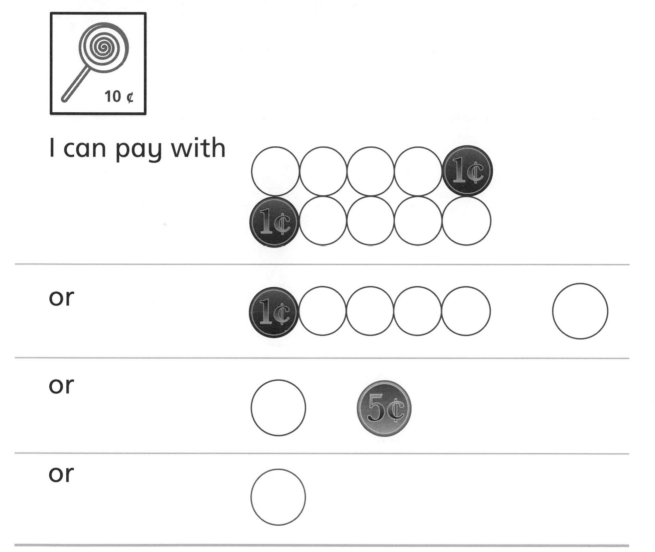

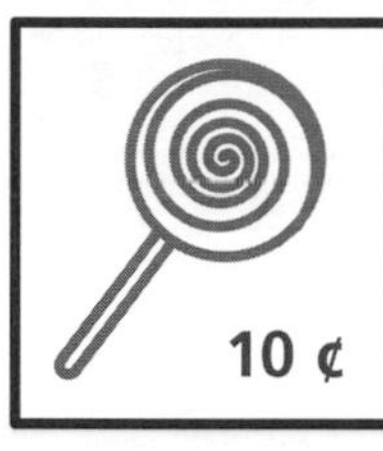

I can pay with 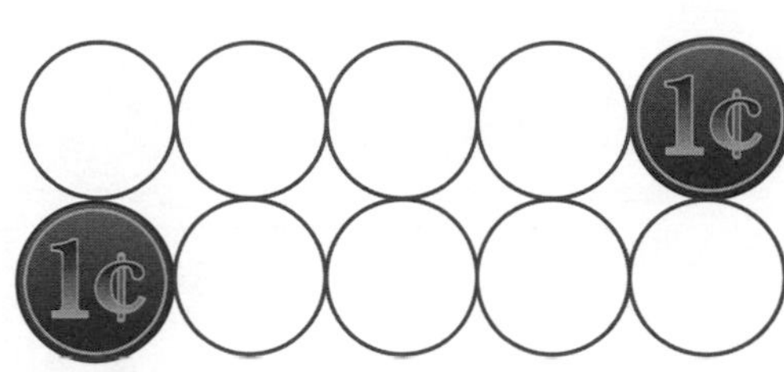

or 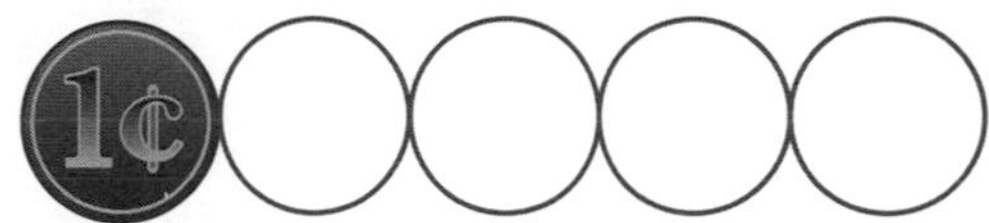 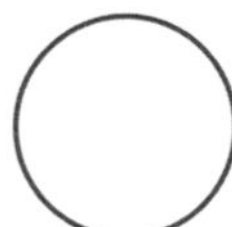

or 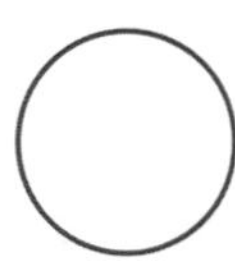 

or 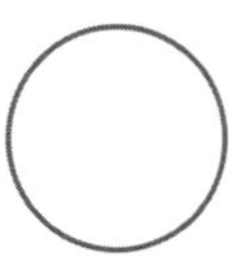

b Draw the coins you need to buy the balloon.

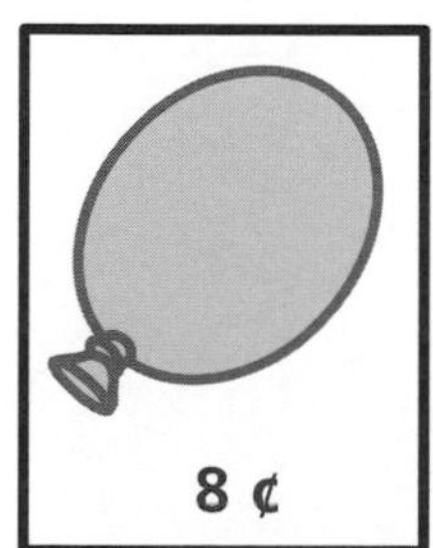

6 Using coins to buy

Draw the coins you need to buy each sticker.

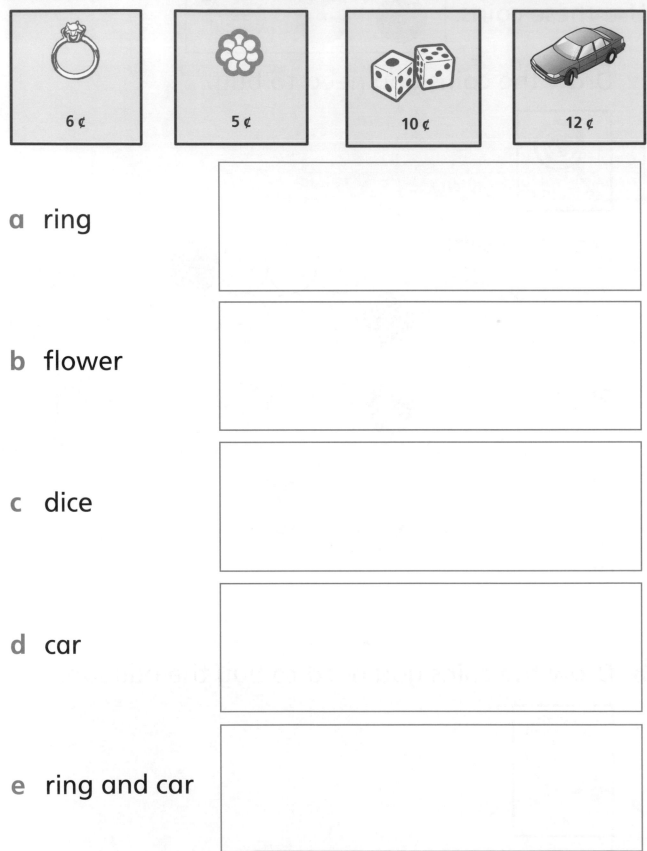

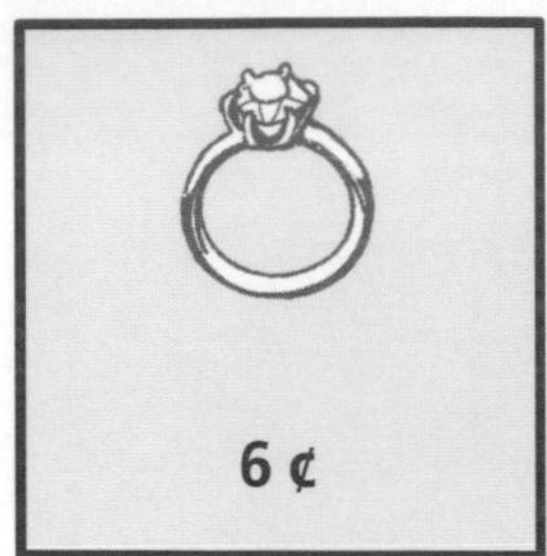 6 ¢	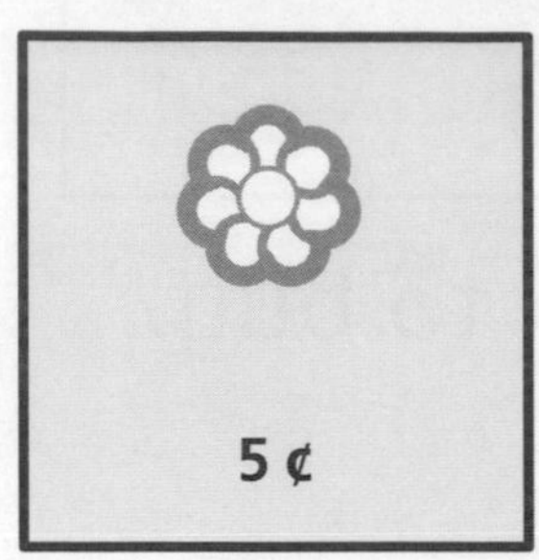 5 ¢	 10 ¢	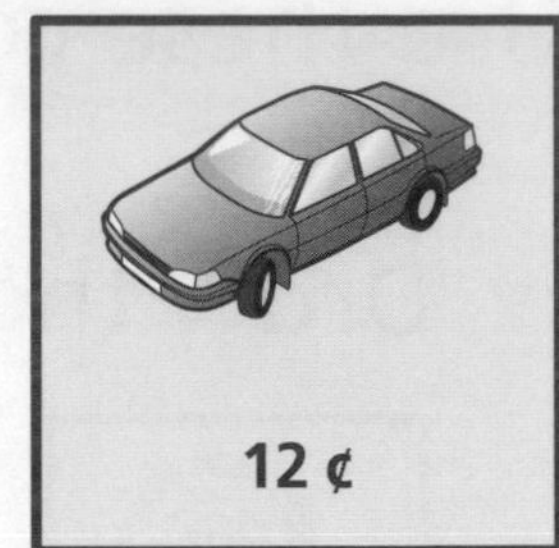 12 ¢

a ring

b flower

c dice

d car

e ring and car

7 Using notes to buy

Draw the notes you need to buy each item.

$ 5

$ 7

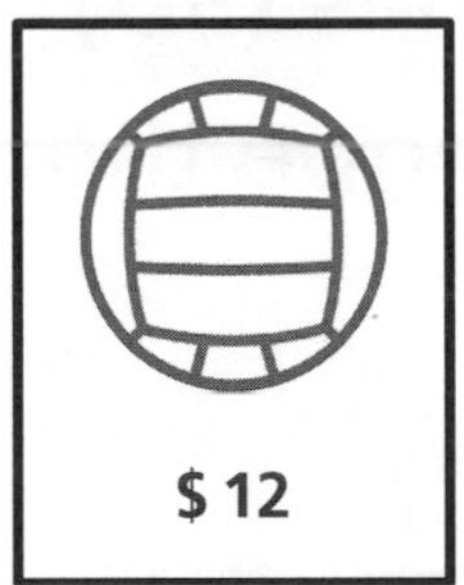

$ 12

$ 10

a ball

b dinosaur

c juice

d ice cream cone

Challenge

Draw the notes you need to buy juice **and** an ice cream cone.

1 Solid shapes (3D)

Colour the shape that is like the one on the left.

a

TISSUES

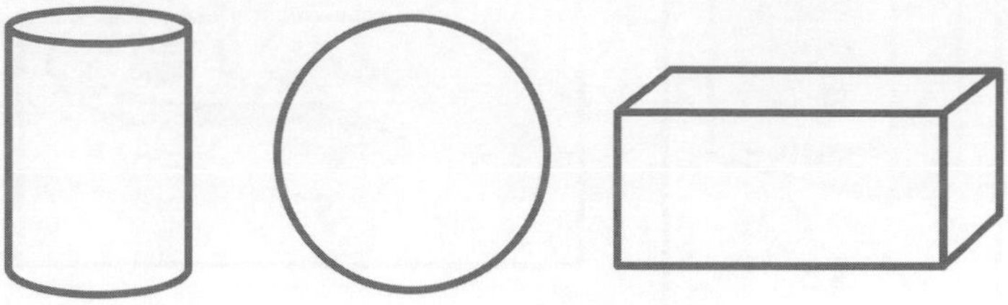

b

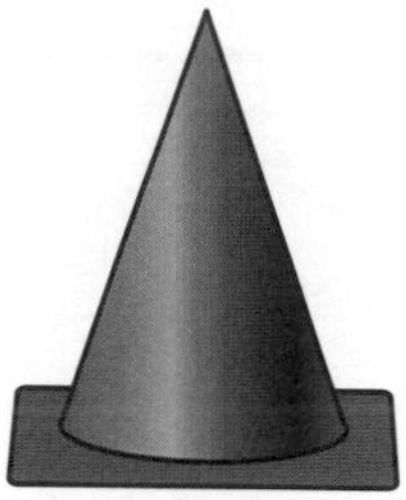

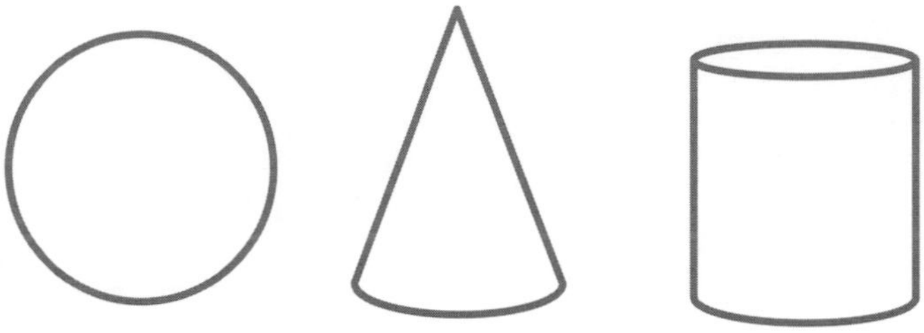

c

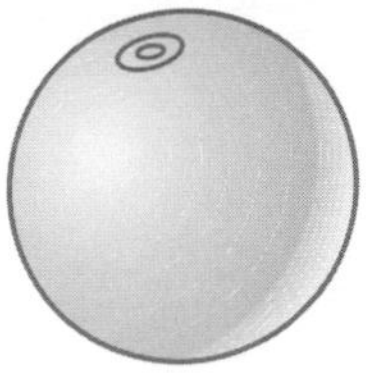

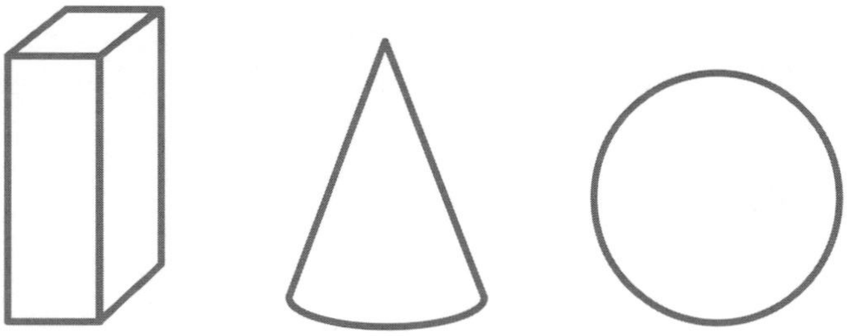

d

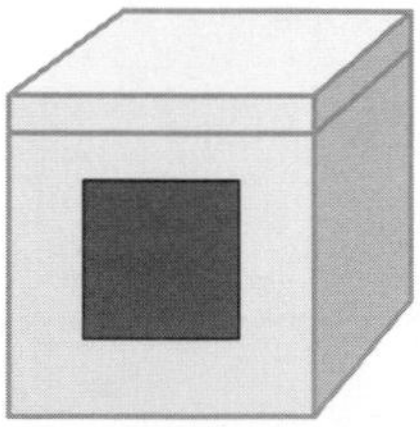

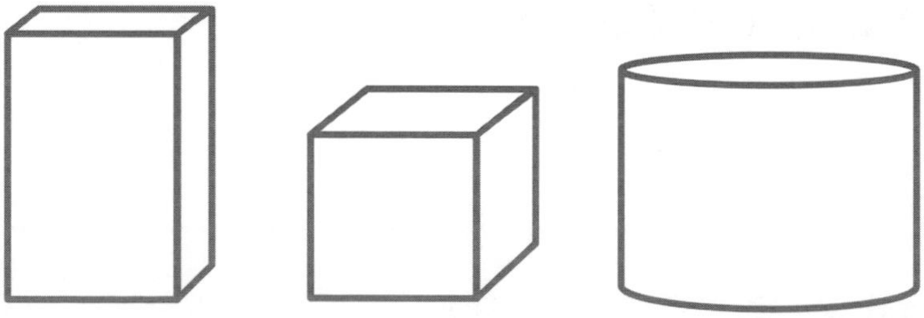

e

BAKED BEANS

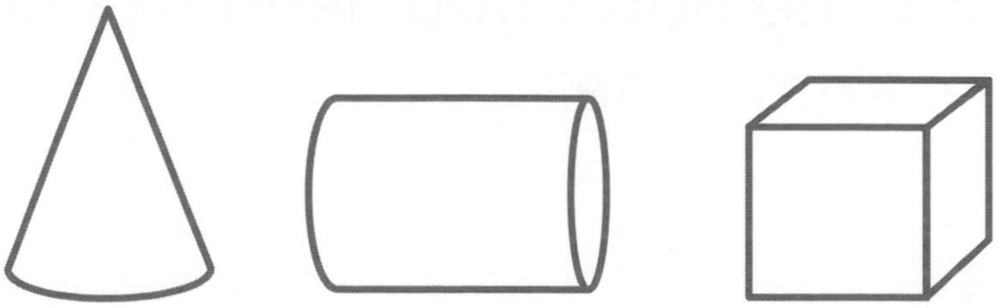

2 Plane shapes (2D): Circles

Colour the circles.

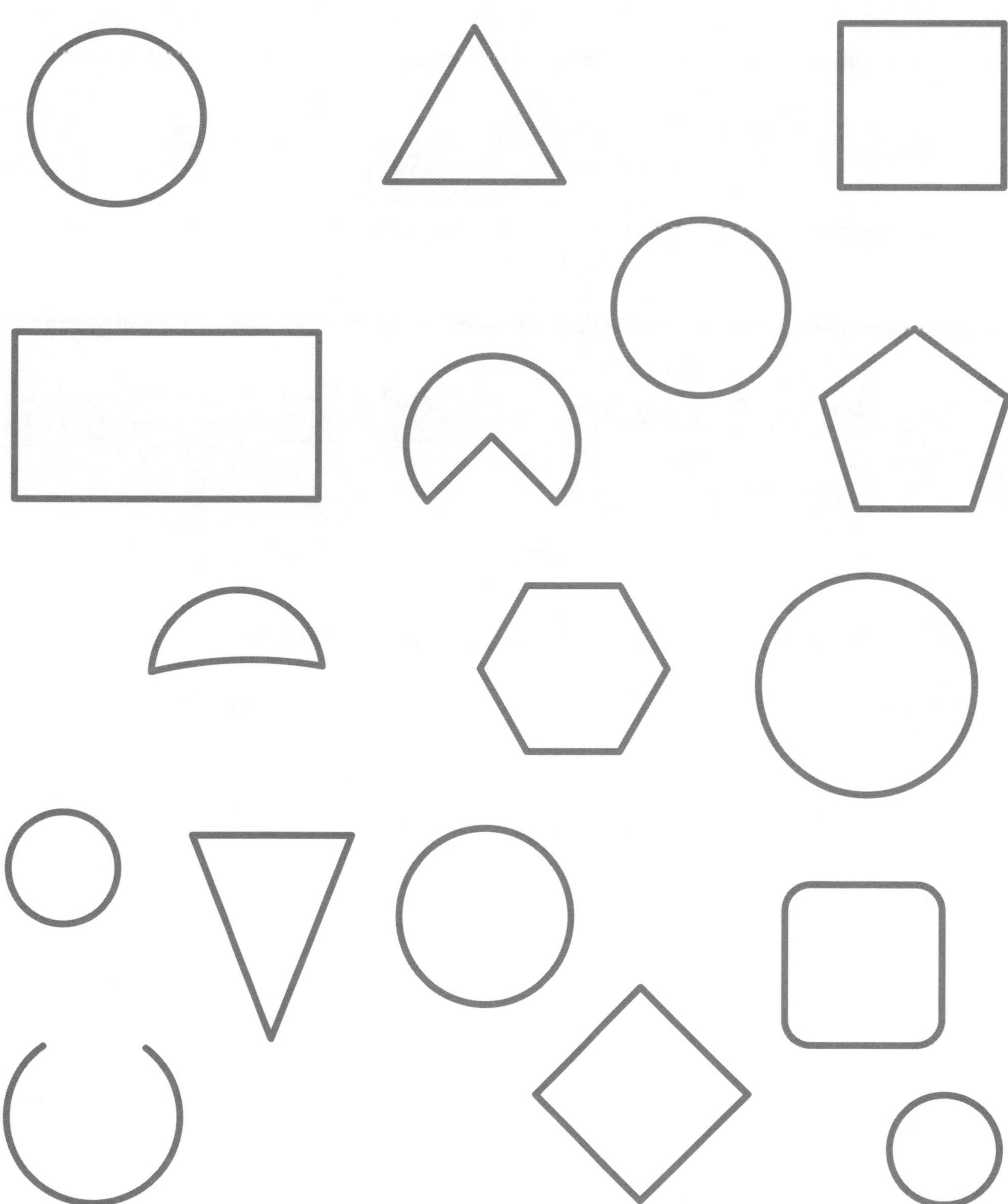

There are ____ circles on this page.

3 Plane shapes (2D): Squares

Outline each square you see in the picture.

a There are ____ squares in the picture.

b Draw a picture that has 5 or more squares.

4 Plane shapes (2D): Rectangles

Colour the rectangles.

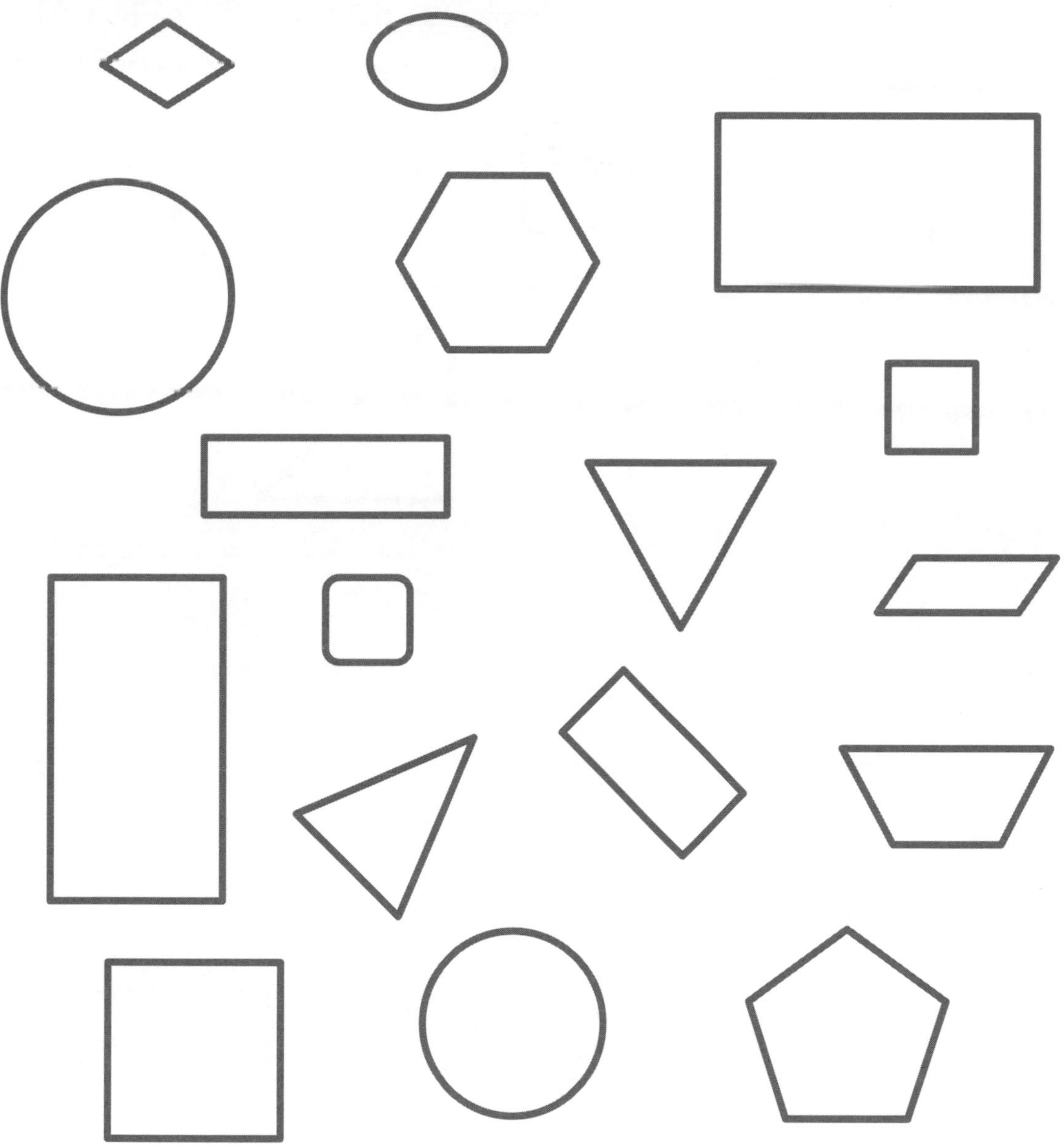

There are ____ rectangles on this page.

Challenge

A square is a special type of rectangle.
Count the squares and the other rectangles.
How many are there altogether? _____

5 Plane shapes (2D): Triangles

Make a picture. Use each triangle one or more times.

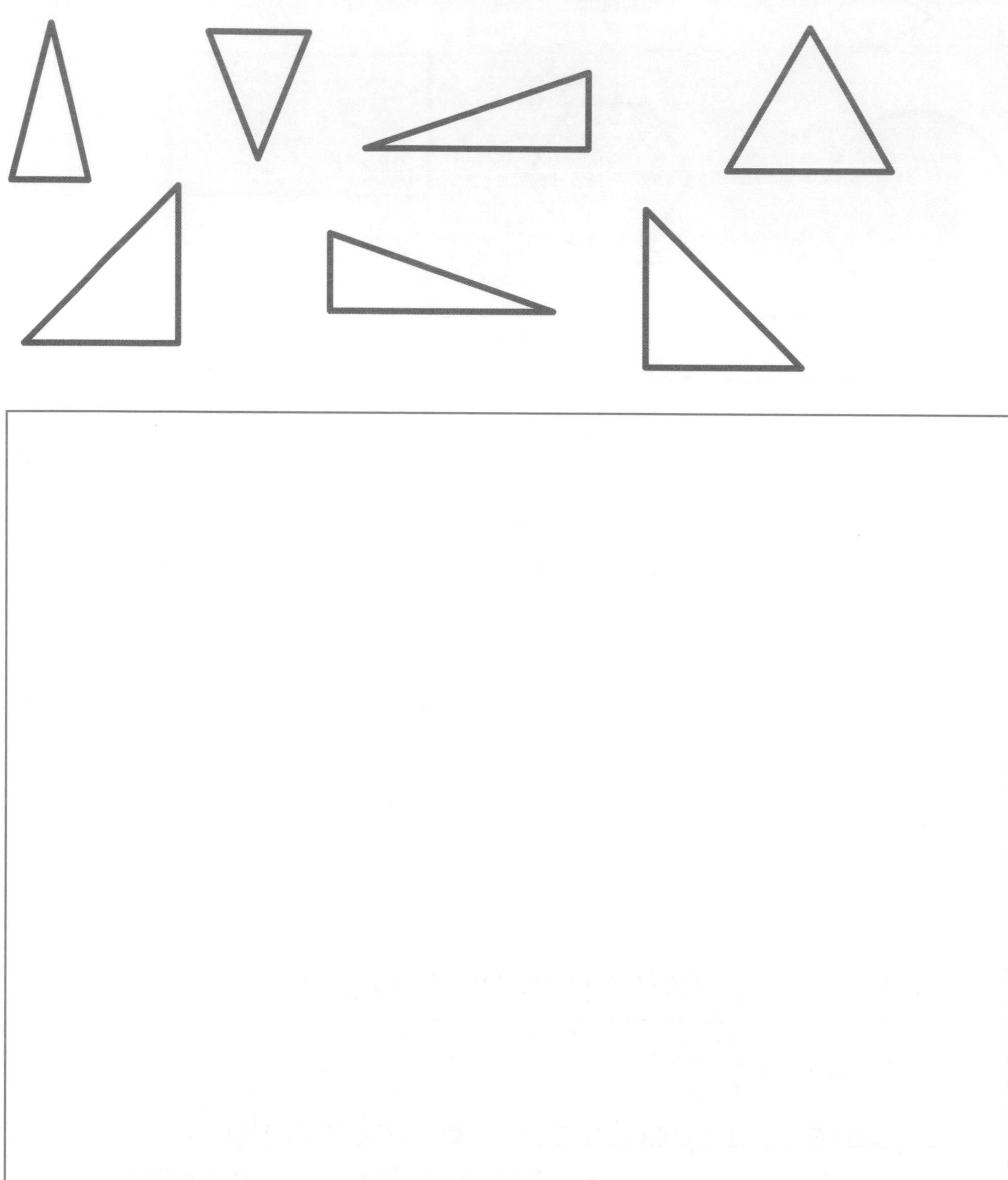

There are ____ triangles in my picture.

6 Symmetry

If you fold the picture or shape on the dotted line, will each side have the same shape? Write yes or no.

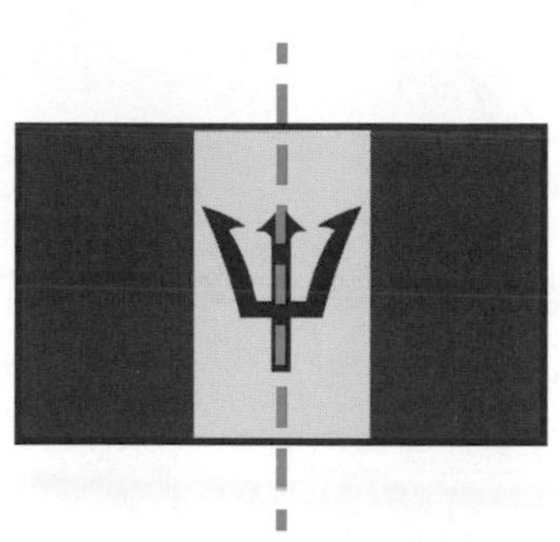

a ____

b ____

c ____

d ____

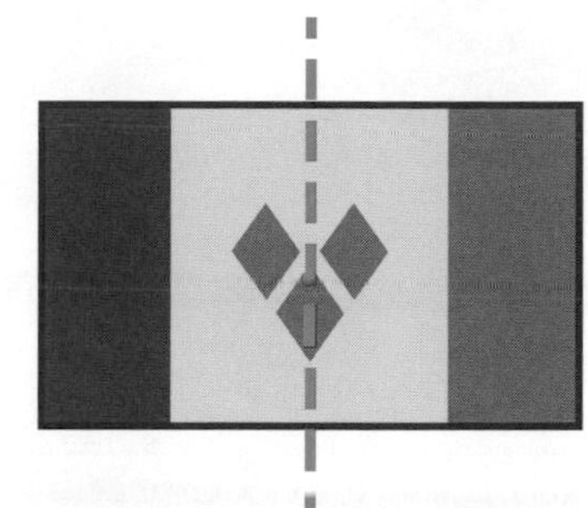

e ____

f ____

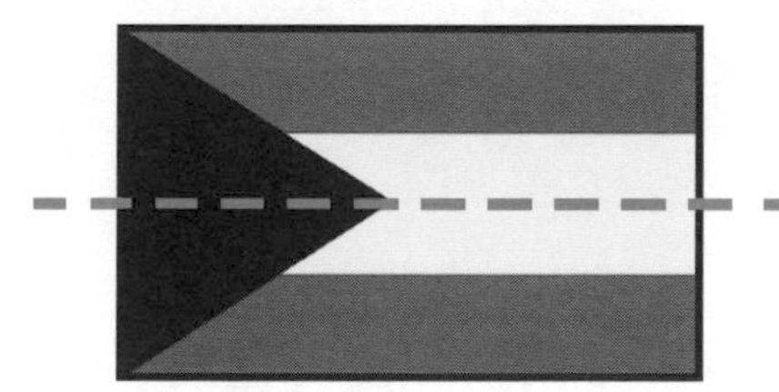

g ____

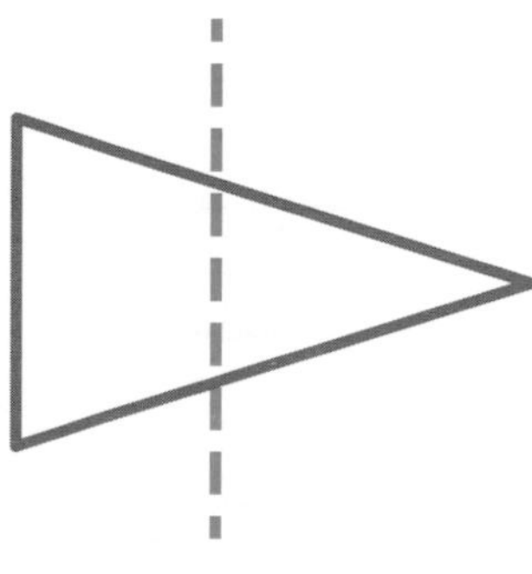

h ____

a 

= ____ ¢

b 

5¢ = ____ ¢

c 

= ____ ¢

d 

$1 = $ ____

e 

$5 = $ ____

f 

$10 = $ ____

g 

$5 = $ ____

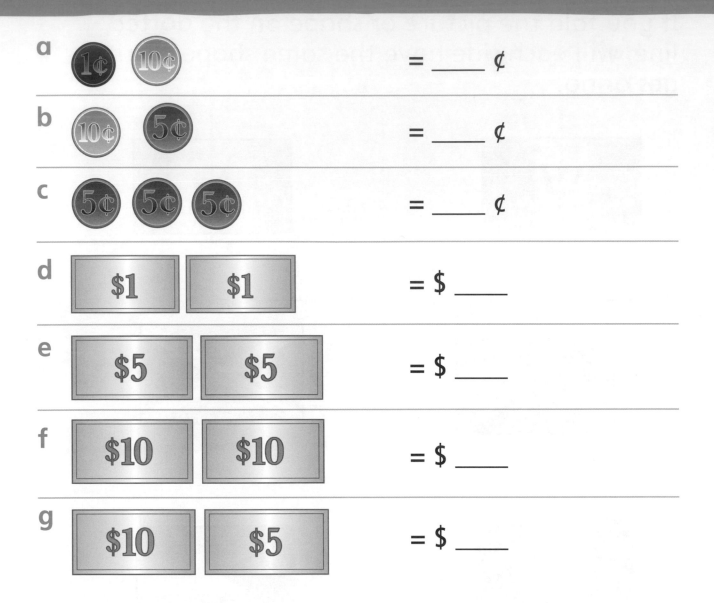

Circle the shape that matches the shape on the left.

h 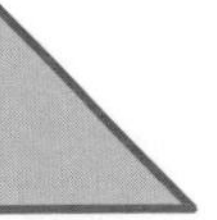 | 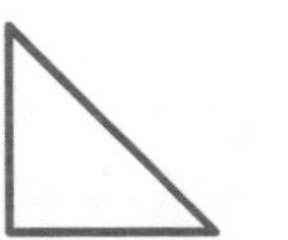 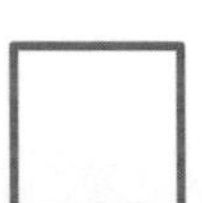

i 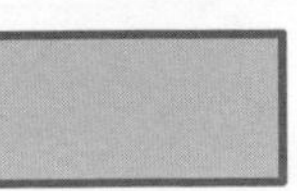 |  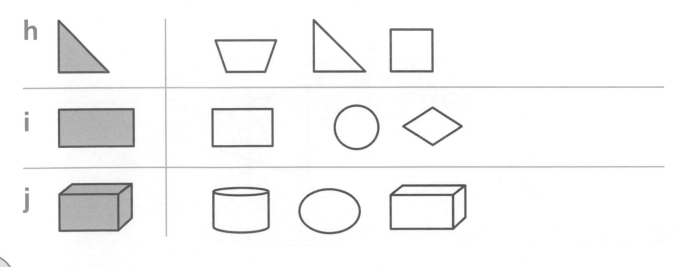

j 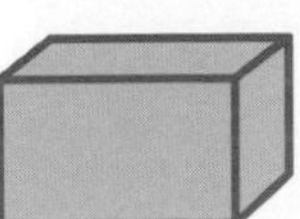 |  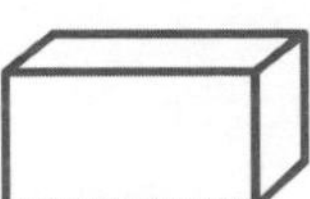

Unit 7: Fractions

1 Half of a set

Circle half of each set.

a 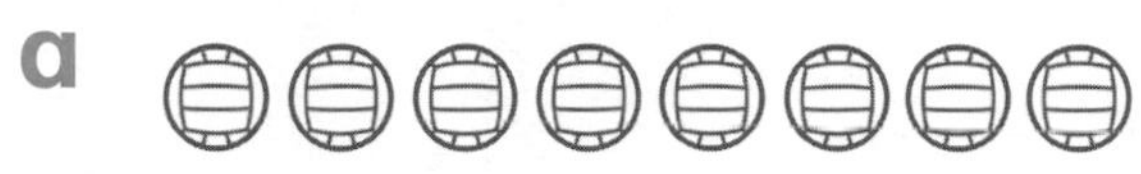

d 

b 

e 

c 

f 

Colour half of each set.

g 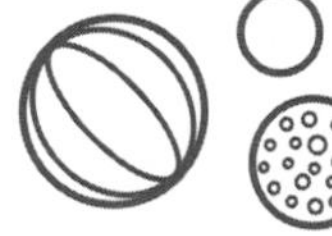 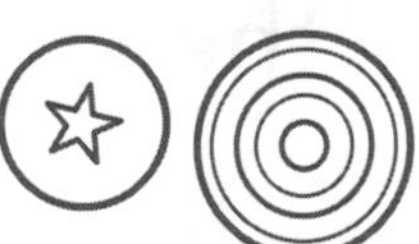

i 

h  

j 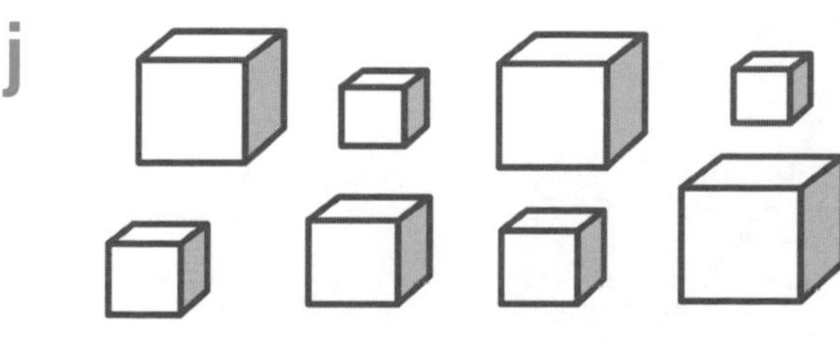

2 Halves

Put a tick ✓ by a shape that shows halves.

Put a ✕ if the dotted line does not make halves in the shape.

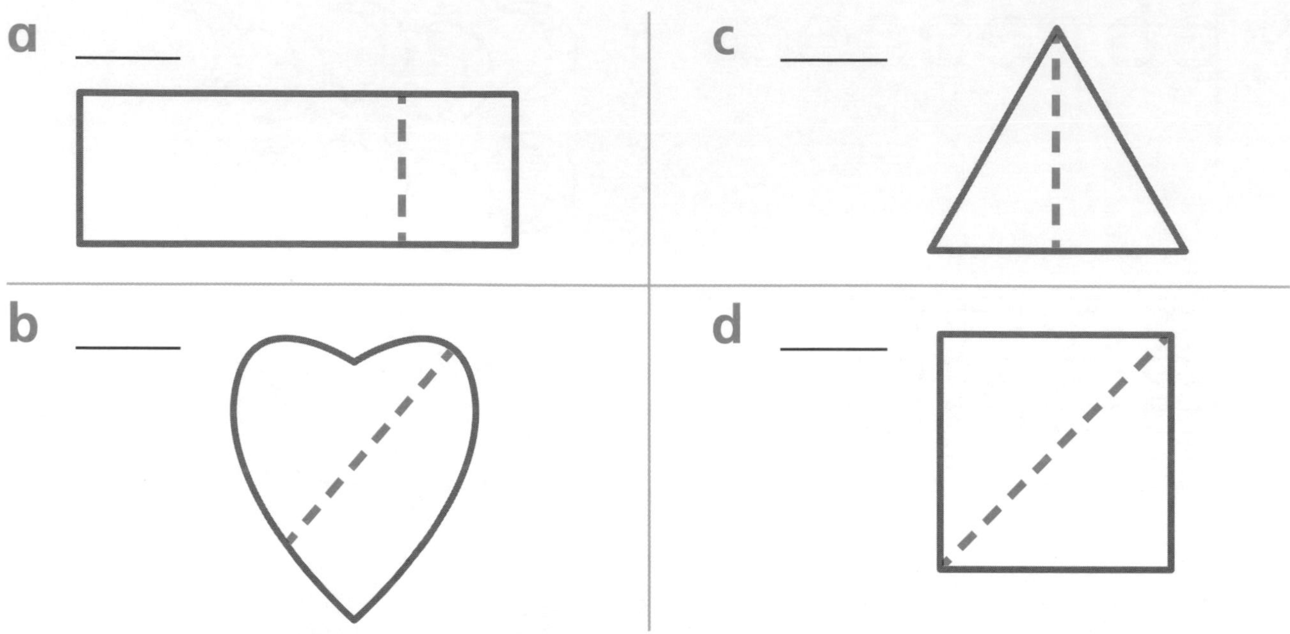

Draw a line to make the shape show halves.

Colour one half of the shape.

e

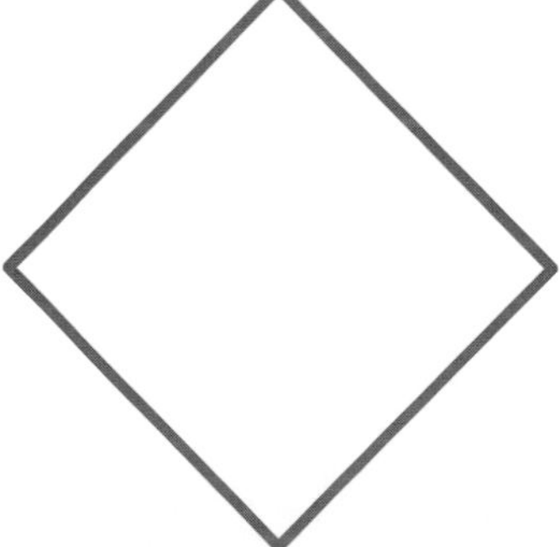

g

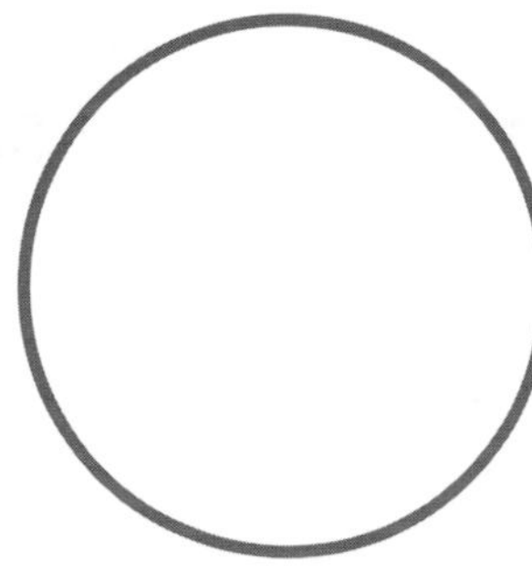

f

h

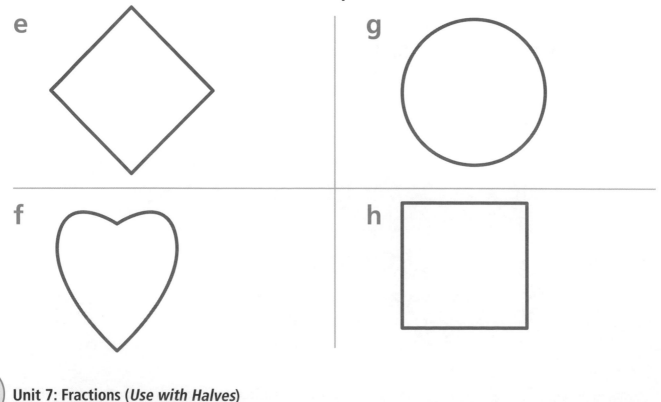

3 Fourths (quarters)

Colour $\frac{1}{4}$ of each shape.

a

d

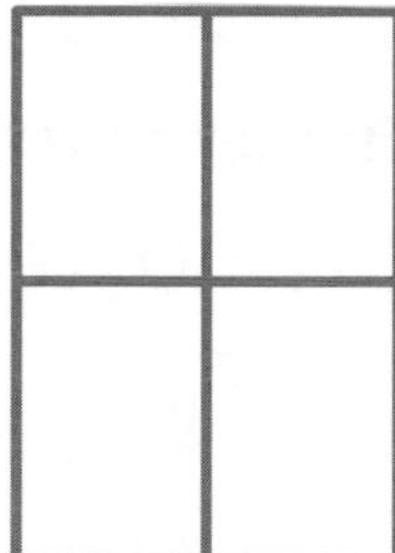

b

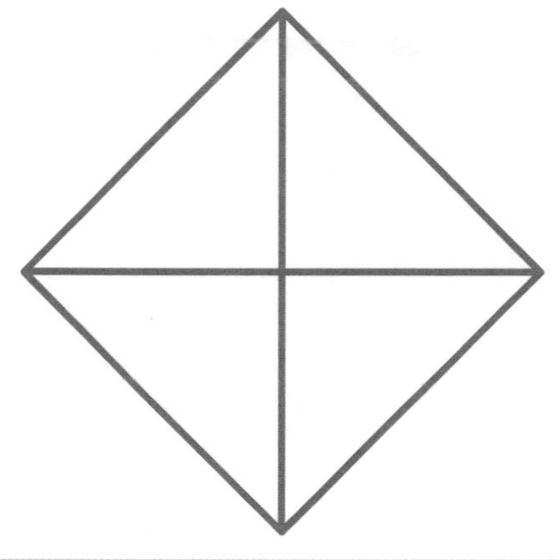

e

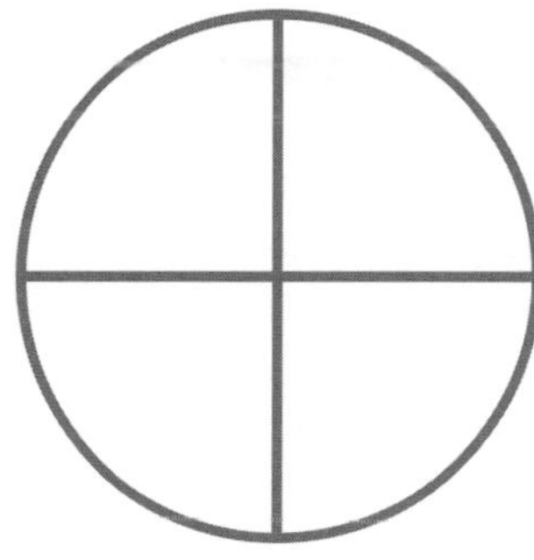

c

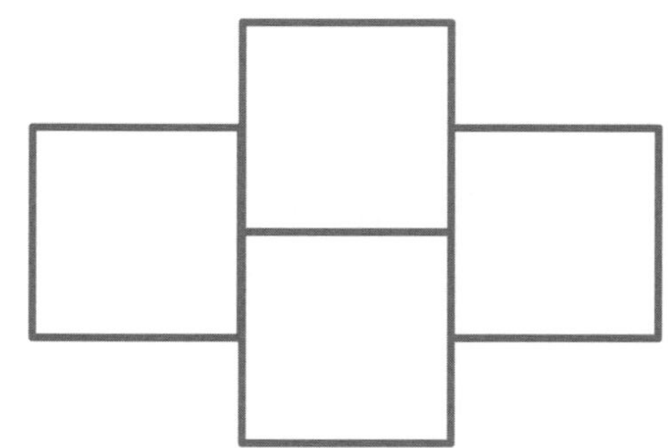

f

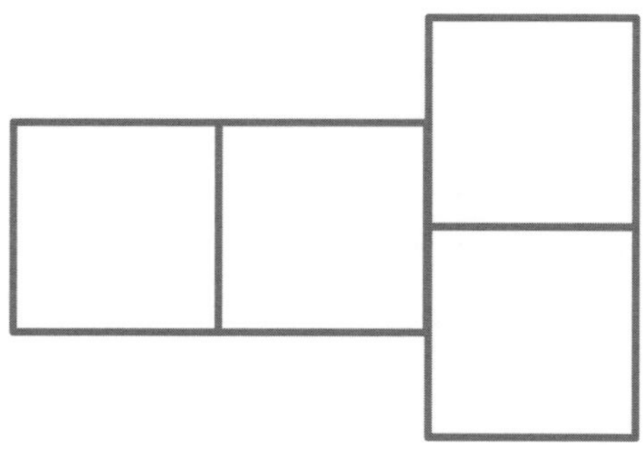

Challenge

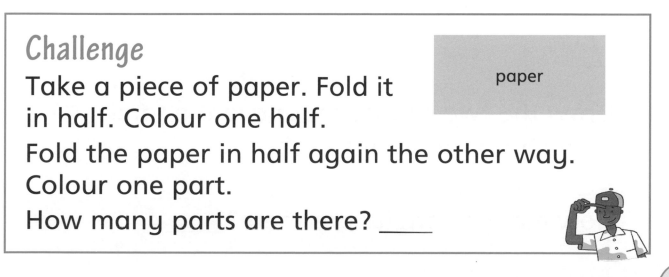

Take a piece of paper. Fold it in half. Colour one half.

paper

Fold the paper in half again the other way. Colour one part.

How many parts are there? ____

1 Making a pictograph

Draw each of these shapes into the graph below.
Cross out each one after you draw it.

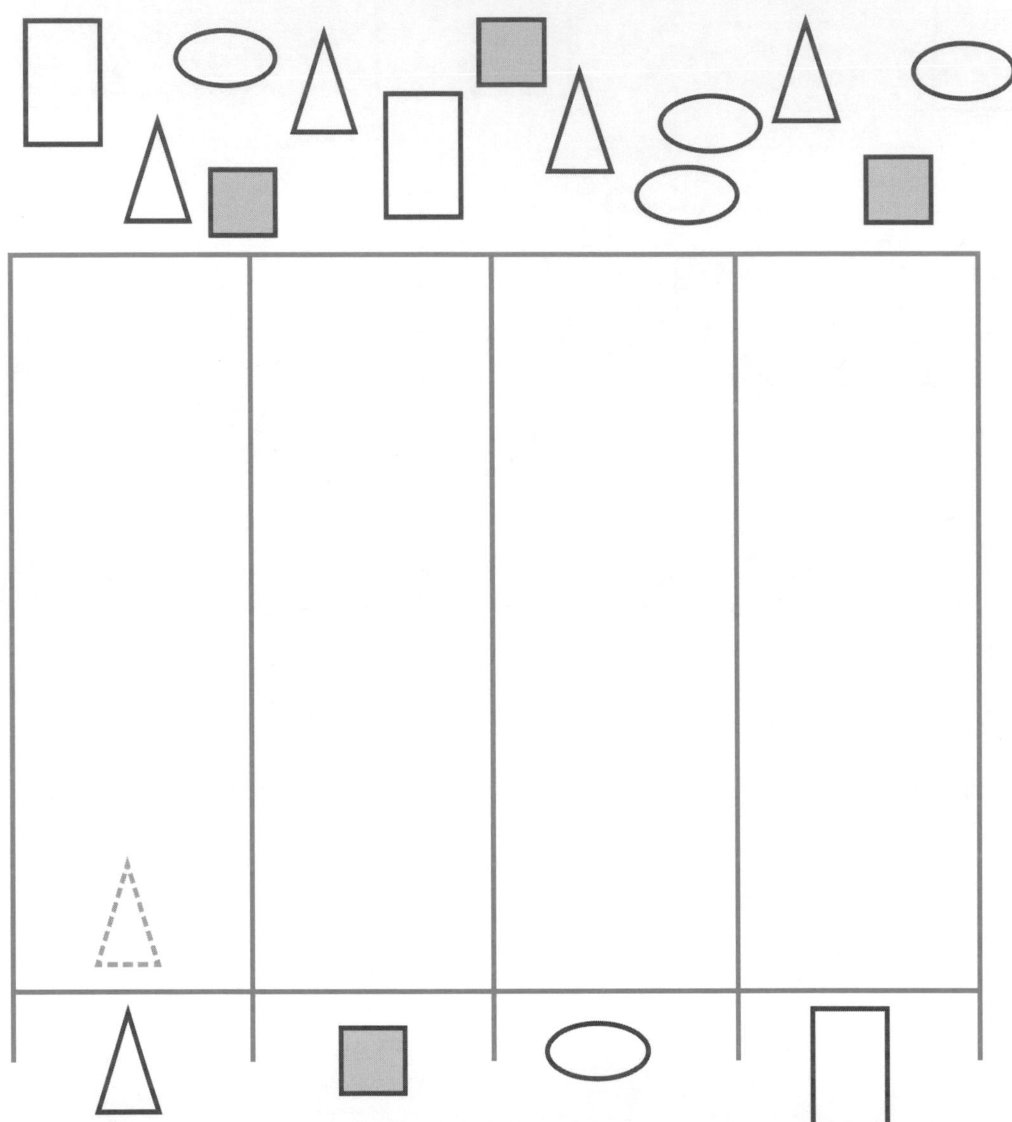

a Draw the two shapes that have the same number on the graph.

____ and ____

b How many triangles are there? ____

2 Reading a bar graph

Look at the graph. It shows the colours of 12 cars.

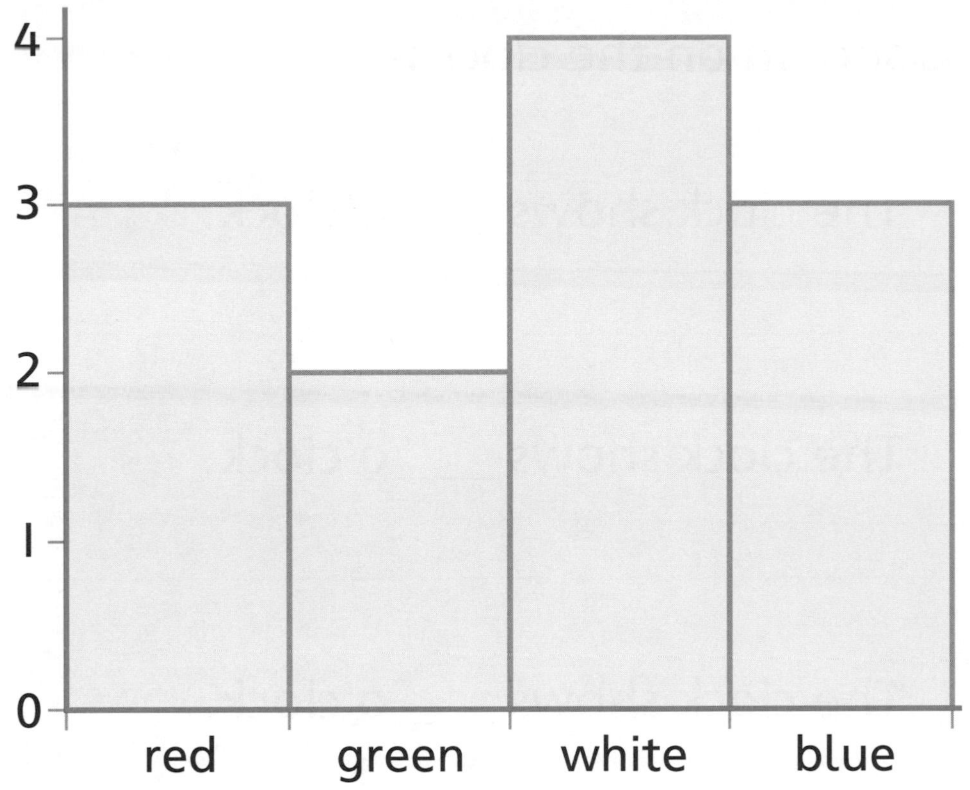

a Most of the cars were (blue / white / red).

b How many white cars were there? ____

c How many cars were green? ____

d The same number of cars were _______ and red.

Count the tally marks and write the totals.

e ~~||||~~ ~~||||~~ = ____

f ~~||||~~ || = ____

---

g Show tally marks for 12.

Unit 9: Measurement

1 Time: o'clock

What time is shown on the clocks?

a

The clock shows ____o'clock.

b

The clock shows ____o'clock.

c

The clock shows ____o'clock.

d

The clock shows ____ o'clock.

Draw hands on the clock to show the time shown:

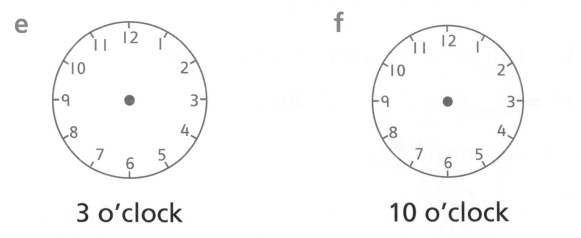

e

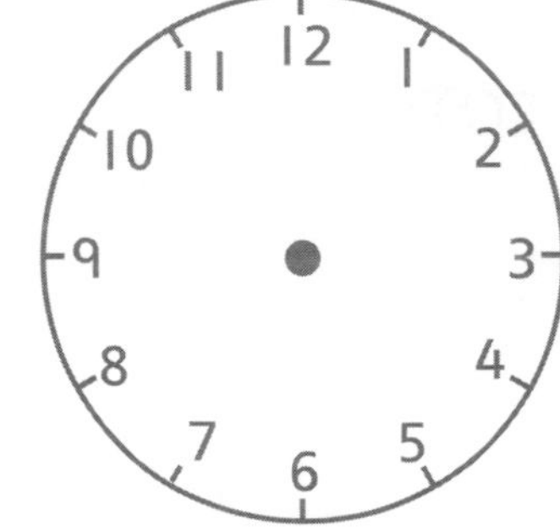

3 o'clock

f

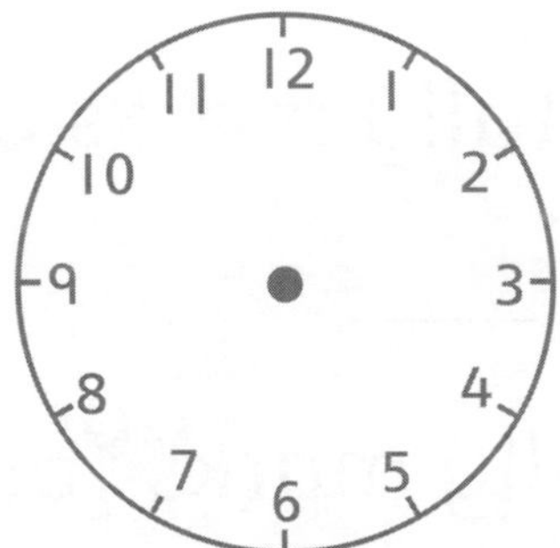

10 o'clock

2 Time: half past

What time is shown on the clocks?

a 

The time is half past ____.

b 

The time is half past ____.

c 

The time is half past ____.

d 

The time is half past ____.

e 

The time is half past ____.

Challenge

I left home at 8 o'clock. I walked for one hour to Papi's house. What time did I get there? Draw it on the clock.

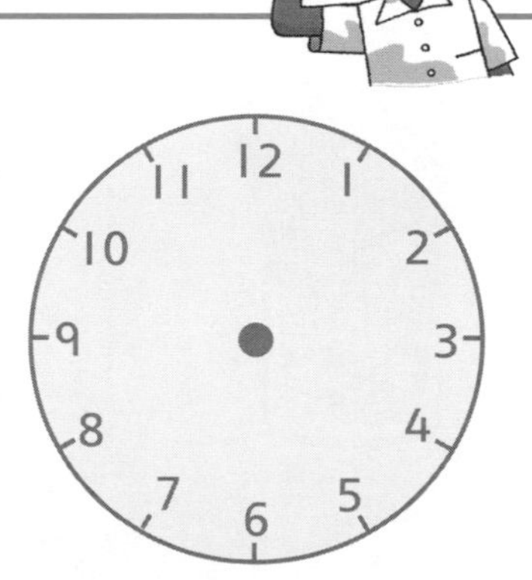

3 Mass: heavier/lighter

Draw something light. Draw something heavy.

a

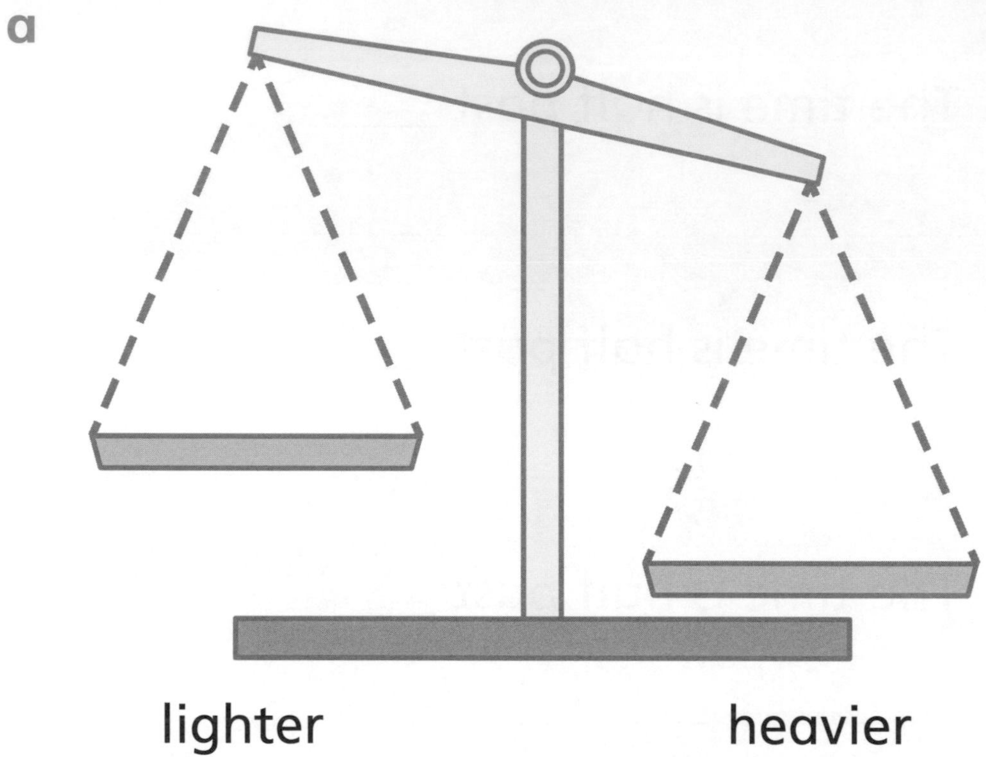

lighter heavier

Circle the side that is heavier.

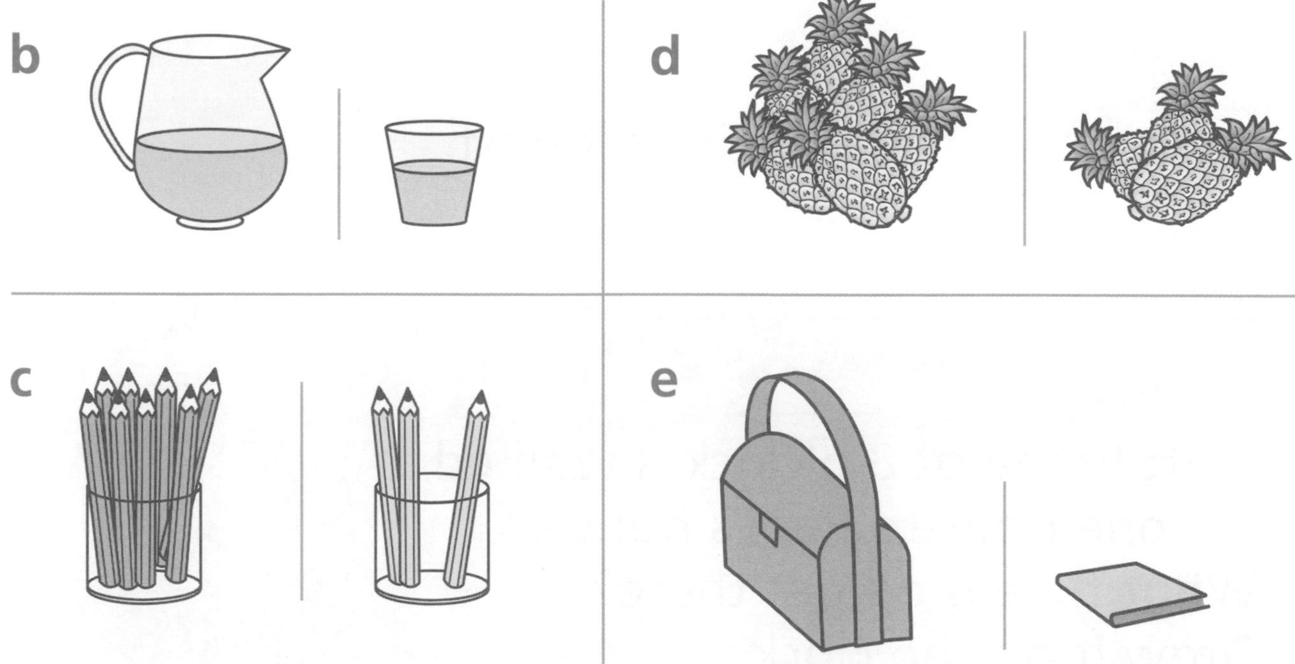

4 Capacity: more or less

a Colour the container that holds more.

b Colour the container that holds less.

Circle more or less.

c

more / less

d

more / less

Challenge

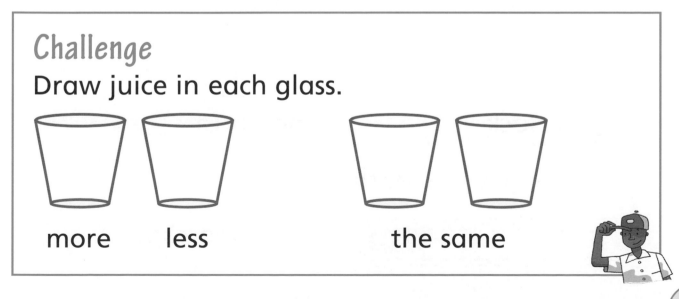

Draw juice in each glass.

more less

the same

1 Count the objects. Circle half the set.

a

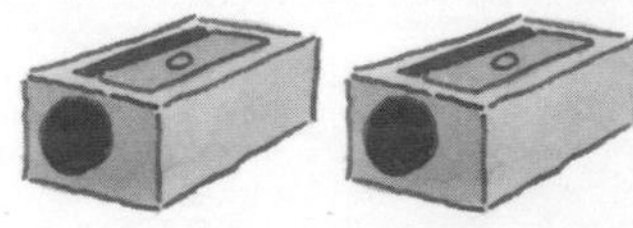

b

2 Colour one fourth (one quarter) of the shape.

a

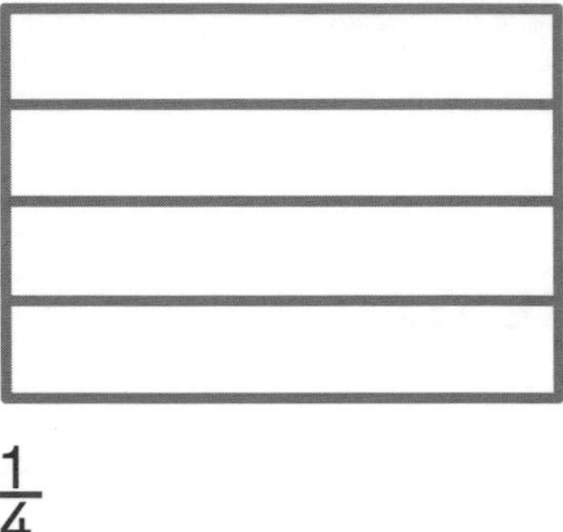

$\frac{1}{4}$

b

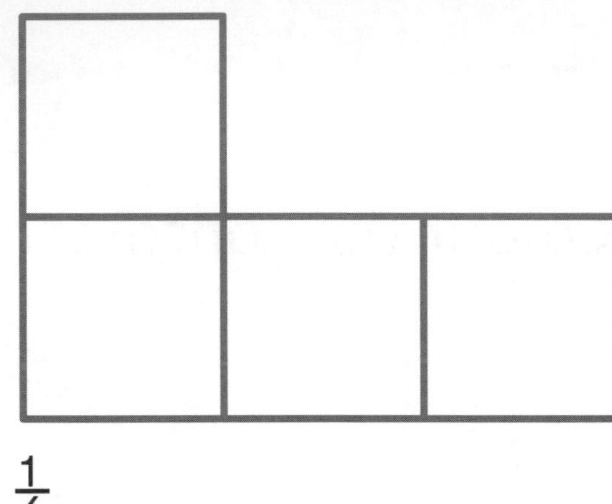

$\frac{1}{4}$

3 How many tally marks?

卌 卌 /// = ____

4 Write the time.

a

____ o'clock

b

half past ____

5 How long is the toothbrush?

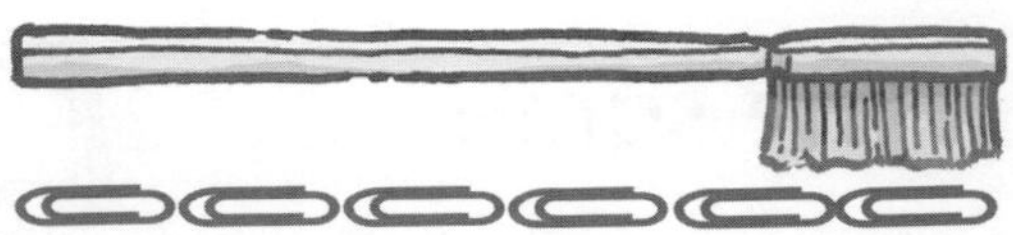

____ paperclips

Unit 10: Building concepts of number

1 Pre-multiplication skills

Circle groups of 2.

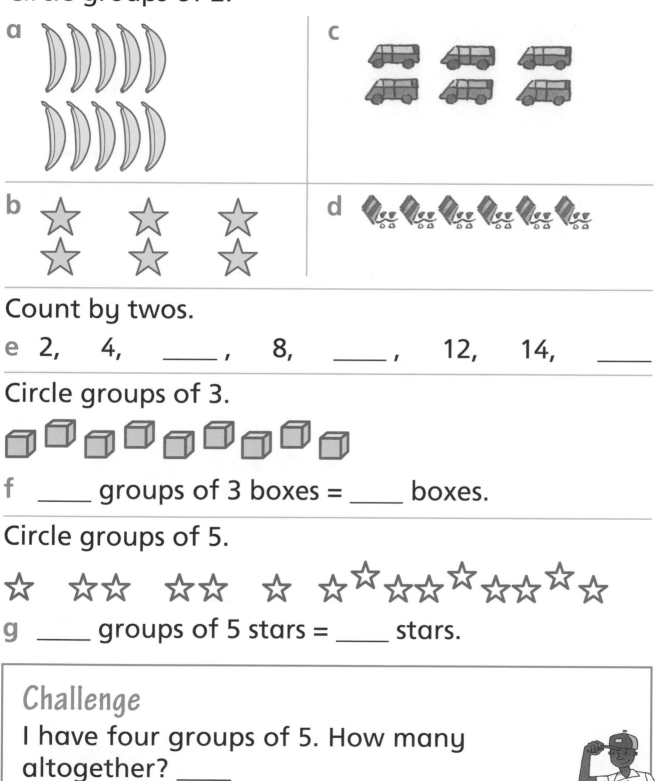

a

b ☆ ☆ ☆ ☆ ☆ ☆

c

d

Count by twos.

e 2, 4, ____ , 8, ____ , 12, 14, ____

Circle groups of 3.

f ____ groups of 3 boxes = ____ boxes.

Circle groups of 5.

☆ ☆☆ ☆☆ ☆ ☆☆☆☆☆☆☆☆☆☆

g ____ groups of 5 stars = ____ stars.

Challenge

I have four groups of 5. How many altogether? ____

2 Tens and ones

How many tens?

a

____ tens = 40

c

____ tens = ________

b

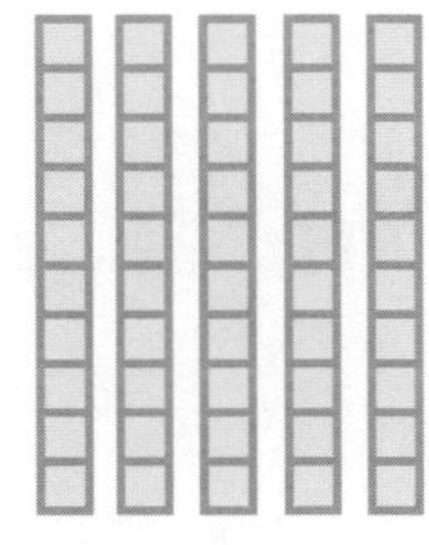

____ tens = ________

d

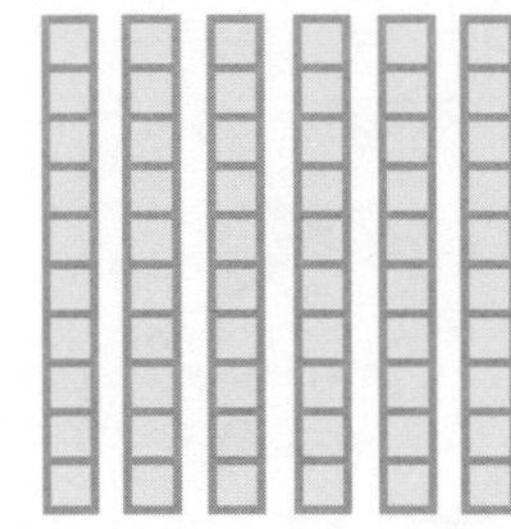

____ tens = ________

How many tens and ones?

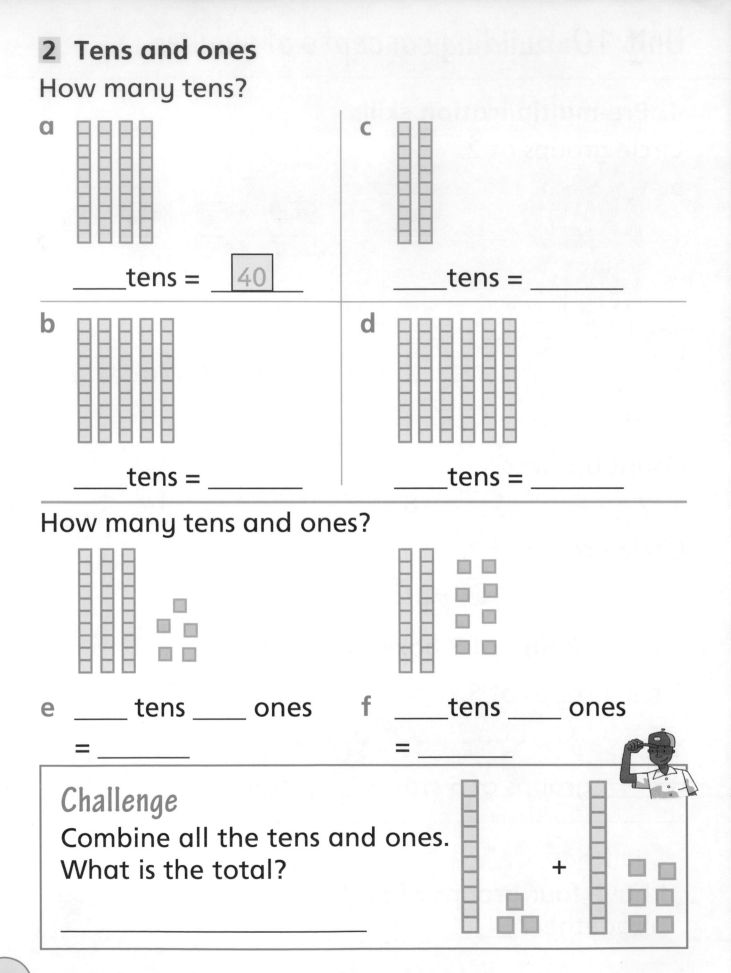

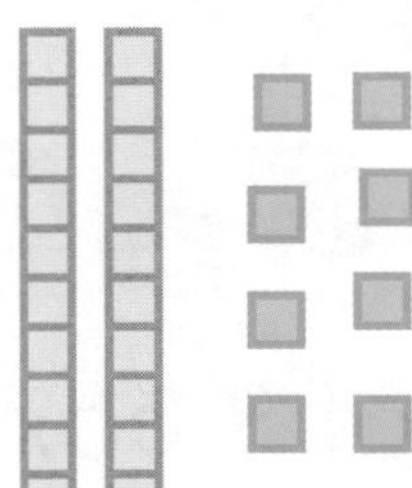

e ____ tens ____ ones

= ________

f ____ tens ____ ones

= ________

Challenge

Combine all the tens and ones.
What is the total?

____

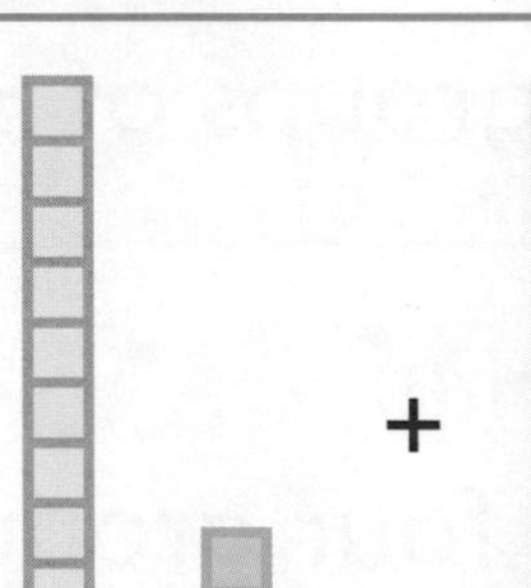